ANCIENT TRADITION

MODERN WARRIOR

Andy Dickinson

Copyright © 2021 Andrew Dickinson

Published by Andrew Dickinson

www.andydickinson.com.au

The moral right of the author has been asserted.

For quantity sales or media enquiries, please contact the publisher at the website address above.

ISBN: 978-0-6484350-2-0 (paperback)

978-0-6484350-3-7 (ebook)

Proofreading by Bill Harper

Cover Design by Miladinka Milic

Design and formatting by Jodi Webster, Vojo Creative

Publishing Consultant Linda Diggle

All rights reserved. Except as permitted under the Australian Copyright Act 1968 (for example, a fair dealing for the purposes of study, research, criticism or review), no part of this book may be reproduced, stored in a retrieval system, communicated or transmitted in any form or by means without written permission. All inquiries should be made to the publisher at the above address.

Disclaimer: Although the authors and publisher have made every effort to ensure the information in this book was correct at press time, the authors and publisher do not assume and hereby disclaim any liability to any party for any loss, damage, or disruption caused by errors or omissions, whether such errors or omissions result from negligence, accident, or any other cause.

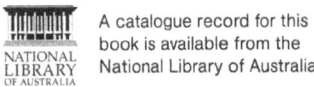 A catalogue record for this book is available from the National Library of Australia

Dedicated to my late father
Alan George Dickinson,
I miss you Dad.

Contents

Testimonials	1
Introduction	5
Breakfalls	37
Rear Collar Grab	38
Single Neck Grab	40
Basic Grabs	41
Bear Hug. Arms Free	44
Bear Hug. Pinned	46
Double Lapel Grab	48
Double Neck Grab	50
Head Lock Basic	53
Head Lock	54
Head Lock. Reverse	56
Rear Bear Hug	58
Rear Collar Grab Outside	61
Front Kick Defence	63
Punch Defence	65
Rear Bear Hug. Pinned	67
Neck Grab	70

Double Shirt Grab. Aiki — 71

Double Wrist Grab — 73

Single Wrist Grab — 74

Ground Flow — 75

Single Shirt Grab — 77

Head Lock to Ground — 80

Knee Defence — 83

Knee to Throw — 86

Side Kick Take Down — 89

Kick Defence — 92

Sparring Drill. — 95

Punch to take down — 95

Single leg take down — 97

Punch Defence to simple throw — 100

Punch Defence — 102

Strikes — 105

Techniques — 109

Appendix 1 — 117

Appendix 2 — 121

Appendix 3 — 132

Acknowledgements — 135

About the Author — 137

Testimonials

"A remarkable person, Andy Dickinson's important contributions and inspirational leadership have not gone unnoticed. Bringing together classical tradition with contemporary insight, this martial arts master has succeeded in linking together defensive functionality with physical fitness and holistic awareness into an exciting transformative pathway of practice. The true warrior spirit transcends the mere physical and becomes as much a product of one's art as the art becomes a product of one's life. Against a backdrop of modern Japanese Ju-jutsu, this is a wonderfully challenging pathway, conditioning the body, cultivating the mind and nurturing the spirit; A life- changing journey... it is the warrior's way!"

Patrick McCarthy
マカシー パトリック
Hanshi 9th Dan
範士九段
International Ryukyu Karate-jutsu Research Society
http://www.koryu-uchinadi.com

"A brilliant road map to enlightenment and a brilliant guide to mastering Ju Jitsu!"

Tom Cronin
Coach, Meditation, Author, Filmmaker

"A lifetimes journey of learning training teaching mentoring and being a solid curator of Budo- Sensei Andy's thorough and extremely practical applications and techniques gives the reader an insight to the quality and effectiveness of the martial arts."

David Nowland
6th Dan blackbelt Sydney Academy of Taekwondo

"I had the pleasure of meeting Andy's late father Alan George Dickinson, whom this book is dedicated to. I've known Andy in excess of 30 years through our association in the classical martial arts of Japan. I have followed Andy's journey since, both in Australia and Japan. Not only has he had the unique opportunity to have studied two koryu jūjutsu traditions throughout his life to a high level of skill, he and has also received diplomas of proficiency in Tenjin Shinyō Ryū jūjutsu (Kubota Toshihiro sensei) and Daitō Ryū Aikijūjutsu (Kondo Katsuyuki sensei) rarely seen outside Japan.

He has continued a thorough study of theory and techniques of Jūdō and Submission arts wrestling, Taekwondo and Thai Kick boxing in Japan, South Korea and Thailand respectively and officially approved methods of hand to hand combat in addition to the koryū jūjutsu to protect oneself against civil social disorder. During the studies of this shinbudō he has displayed combat morality with a strong spiritual discipline and proper technique in both armed and unarmed combat, as well as his individual development of physical and psychological health.

Today, jūjutsu is probably one of the most misinterpreted martial arts in the world. Commonly, in the western world the original meaning of the term jūjutsu has been defined erroneously, and its practical use extensively modified or exaggerated to fit in with the social needs and wants of the public for the sporting arena. Contrary to popular belief, jūjutsu is not just an unarmed martial art. The historical truth about jūjutsu is based on facts and evidence of its various ancient traditions called the ryū. However one tries to denote it, Andy explains exactly what jūjutsu is or isn't. As he states in his book, 'History tells us'.

This insightful man continues his in-depth study and practise of jūjutsu by retaining a true connection as a disciple within the martial arts where he maintains the old classical warrior virtues. In this modern world, Andy's method of jūjutsu is as binding today as it was in Japan during the days of yore.

He ticks all the right boxes. Education and training are the answer. He's a man of perseverance and has exhaustively studied the principles of jūjutsu and the spiritual martial way. Read his book but think about it methodically. Andy can support what he says, not just with words and pictures in this book which only touch the surface, but also through his life experiences.

It is enlightening to be in Andy's company to listen and watch regarding his knowledge and practical understanding in the art of jūjutsu. I'm honoured and humbled to be associated with him.

He has certainly rendered a distinguished service (Kōrō) regarding the education and training in the art of jūjutsu both old style and new style to many people throughout Australia and overseas."

Philip Hinshelwood
Yagyū Shingan Ryū Heihōjutsu (jūjutsu)
Kyodensho Chikuosha
Australia, 2021.

"I am very happy to endorse this book of Andy's on Ju Jitsu. As in yoga and meditation, my own area of experience, it is essential to connect with the tradition, and noble intent that comes with that. It is not sufficient to learn any martial skill without imbibing the principle and purpose at the same time. In a sense Ju Jitsu and meditation are alike in that they both aim at knowledge of and mastery of oneself. And it is clear that Andy's intention in this book is to make the case to return the martial art to its rightful intent and purpose.

So I'm happy to leave the last word to Andy which makes that intent clear and to the point:

It may seem paradoxical that by learning to fight we no longer want to fight."

Swami Anandakumar
Teacher of Meditation

Introduction

Andy Dickinson

Ju Jitsu. Ancient tradition – modern warrior

It's been a wonderful journey putting together my thoughts, theories and techniques for this book. But I don't want you to think that my putting them all in a book means it's an end product.

Because nothing could be further from the truth.

The photos of these techniques are a snapshot in time - a single reference point in a 40-year timeline. I'm still learning and developing in so many ways.

I was lucky to find all these photos in a forgotten box in the corner of a storage unit. They mark a significant period of growth, and are an important milestone in my martial arts journey.

I'm often asked what kind of martial arts I teach. And I'm always hesitant to answer as it then defines both me and my system. These days I just say "Ju Jitsu", but my system of Ju Jitsu can't be pigeonholed. It's complex in its uniqueness, and doesn't resemble any other form of Ju Jitsu. Having studied Jujutsu heavyweights Daito Ryu Aiki Ju Jutsu and Tenjin shin yo ryu Ju Jujutsu, my Ju Jitsu is infused with many of their famous techniques, and then integrated with modern judo, taekwondo and Thai boxing for completeness.

As you read on, I hope you will begin to see the beauty of my system. I am simply a transmitter of knowledge. The real work was done in the beginning, when the ancient teachings and their worthiness were tested by the sword against the sword.

My first introduction to Ju Jitsu was a short clip in a spy movie called The Osterman Weekend starring Craig T Nelson and Rutger Hauer back in 1984. Thinking back now, it wasn't a great example of Ju Jitsu. But it did plant a seed in my mind and I just had to find out more.

Three years later I was on my way to train in a style of Ju Jutsu in Tokyo, Japan that would change my life. I didn't consider myself a beginner, as I already had a second dan in taekwondo and a first dan in another Japanese Ju Jutsu system.

But I soon found out how little I really knew.

I understand this book may go totally against your understanding of what Ju Jitsu is. The argument of what came first—Brazilian Jiu Jitsu (BJJ) or Japanese Ju Jitsu—can't be applied here, as history tells us Japanese Ju Jitsu is the original form. This is in no way a criticism of BJJ, but I want to make it very clear that BJJ was influenced primarily by judo, which is also a hybrid of traditional Japanese Ju Jitsu.

As a martial artist, it's easy to fall into the trap of using the lessons merely as a path for self-defence or sport. That's fine in the beginning, but as you develop, your instructor's limitations may leave you stuck in your comfort zone and wondering what comes next.

The chance of you having to use your martial arts in a real physical self-defence situation is pretty low. You may need to use it once in your lifetime—twice if you're really unlucky.

Of course, if you're argumentative, angry and aggressive by nature then trouble will always find you. But if your attitude is neutral, light, non-threatening and forgiving, and you actively avoid aggression, you can go for years without ever having to raise your voice.

The real quality of the martial arts experience is you can use the lessons to enhance every aspect of your life. It allows you to keep a cool, calm head at home and at work during disagreements, arguments, or worse.

But how is this possible when the focus is on learning combat moves for self-defence or competition?

It may seem paradoxical that by learning to fight we no longer want to fight. Some will say it's because you have a new-found confidence, and are more likely to turn the other cheek because you don't want to hurt anyone.

That may be the case, but it's not enough.

No matter what you learn in your dojo, unless you learn to address the behavioural patterns you've had since birth you'll keep acting the way you always have. You won't realise that you can choose whether or not to engage, regardless of your default emotions. And the ability to choose is a by-product of your awareness training in the dojo.

Many martial arts instructors believe the confidence, self-esteem, self-discipline, self-control and other by-products of the physical training are the keys to living a better life. That may seem to work at first, but unless we dig deeper we're all slaves to our default patterns and programming. Teaching how these qualities can be transferred from the dojo to our daily lives would be a good start. There are no secrets here, but we need to go inward to discover the keys to understanding what I'm talking about.

I'm not denying the importance of having a robust effective martial art you can use to defend yourself. After all, we're talking about martial arts. But martial arts can act as the working surface—the point of contact between you and what you are doing—for awareness, and can be applied to any movement.

When you're doing basic moves in the dojo you can give your full attention to the point of contact between the skin and your uniform, your fist and the pad, or the tatami mats and your feet. And you can do the same with the point of contact between your hands and what you touch when you're washing the dishes, or wiping the floor down, or folding the washing. This is the truth behind Mr Miyagi in The Karate Kid when he instructs Daniel san to "Wax on, wax off".

You don't need to run to the top of a mountain and become a monk to tap into your inner warrior. Simply take the lesson of awareness, and life itself will become your dojo.

Becoming a spiritual warrior

I originally had this information at the end of the book. But then I realised that for you to get the most out of your martial arts journey I should share it sooner rather than later.

I'm writing all of this from personal experience. My life is in calm waters now, and I live a quiet meditative life where my wife Liz and I can walk to the water's edge and gently contemplate life and its many mysteries.

I need to share this with you now so you can avoid the painful lessons I had to go through to get to where I am now. It may motivate you to see the value in seeking peace rather than suffering as your underlying focus.

As humans, we reflect our inner world onto our outer world. How we live our lives is directly related to what we think. And the world will never change while we keep thinking and acting in terms of "What's in it for me?". Choosing to go inside—meditating, doing mindfulness, seeking therapy and/or studying the scriptures—is the beginning of an inward journey.

Choosing to go inside and meditate isn't for the faint-hearted. You'll come face to face with your biggest opponent: yourself. Your thoughts, feelings and emotions will be laid bare in front of you. Becoming a spiritual warrior is about developing the courage to look at the things you thought were a reality for you, taking ownership of them, and changing for the better.

I used to have a lot of anger, and was quite jealous of others' success. I was short-tempered and impatient. Over the years I've been meditating. By taking the focus off my thoughts as the driver, and watching them against a backdrop of conscious awareness, the power of the negative behaviour has lost its impact.

But I didn't just replace one thought with another because that never works. In martial arts we have a saying: The sword cannot cut itself. It basically means the thinking ego-mind can't change by adding more thinking, as it's actually the source of the problem.

Just learning to meditate isn't the answer either. If you're not careful, it can become just another pattern of thinking. The ego-mind is very sneaky, and so you constantly need to refresh it by auditing your behaviour, questioning your motives, and asking whether this way of thinking still serves you. This takes courage and effort. A leopard may never change its spots, but real and lasting change on the inside is possible.

So you have a choice. The world as you see it will only be at peace if you choose and live with peace inside yourself. This doesn't mean turning the other cheek, but rather creating the space in your life to see that in every interaction you have a choice. You can act as you always have, or be the spiritual warrior and choose a response that makes you feel better and shows empathy for others.

Welcome to a different world. Choose peace.

The master's way

Over the years I've come to realise that we really don't know very much. As much as we try to think, analyse, and justify our knowledge, the real wisdom and depth of understanding comes with just feeling.

To experience this, we need to get ourselves out of the way and allow the lessons to arise within us. The feeling we often call our 'gut feeling' is rarely wrong.

In this book I present a series of moves and their defences. Each move is just one interpretation of what's possible, and there are plenty of other ways to do the defensive moves. For each move I provide a narrative on why I perform the defensive move the way I do. But while I think it's useful, I understand that you may not agree with what I say. In the words of the famous Bruce Lee, take what's useful and discard the rest. Most of the moves I present have evolved and been assimilated into my current Ju Jitsu system, Northstar Ju Jitsu.

The moves in this book are all dangerous and should be respected, especially the throwing moves. Your attacker probably won't know how to position themselves to take the throw safely. Add to this hard surfaces and other obstacles, and you have a potentially lethal combination. So please proceed with caution. They should only be practised with the utmost care, and ideally under the supervision and guidance of an experienced teacher. (My partner in these moves is my student Kieran O'Connell, an experienced black belt.)

I still think it's strange that learning how to fight can help you become an advocate for peace. But that's exactly what happened to me. I've always taken the attitude that martial arts is a holistic practice that encourages positive growth of the body, mind and spirit. At some stage this may include a meditation practice, which can loosely be described as martial arts of the mind. I've been subtly teaching my martial arts students the art of awareness by gently teaching my classes with a mindful attitude. If and when they're ready, they too may discover the wonderful gift of meditation and awareness.

The martial artist who takes the leap to look at their inner workings will ultimately be able to choose the peaceful option in conflict—not the easier option. It means they'll be less likely to be drawn into conflict.

Now I'm not saying you shouldn't defend yourself. What I'm saying is the mark of a true martial arts master is being able to see exactly what's needed, and then using just enough force to defend themselves once they decide to act. The path to this understanding and wiser option is a by-product of an evolved, mindful approach to awareness.

I've spent the past 40 years developing my body and mind through combat. And I'd do it all again if I had to. I won't say I've loved every minute of it, but the journey of self-discovery has made it worthwhile.

This year I've focused on telling my story online. I've gone back through my archives and gathered as much information as possible so I can share the history and philosophy of the great system of Northstar Ju Jitsu. In doing so, I've been able to relive many great experiences that were almost forgotten.

I've come to realise that my initial drive to study martial arts came from a deep desire to be recognised, and not from the need to learn to defend myself as I initially thought. As a young boy I wasn't very confident, and often felt shamed by my overbearing mother. But although I was bullied and had low self-esteem my body was fit and strong, and relished the physical strength and power my initial martial arts training provided.

I went through my trial by fire in my 20s and early 30s, and enjoyed the recognition that came my way. I felt uneasy that I wasn't living my truth, but back then I wasn't sure what my truth actually was. Defining your truth and purpose can't be rushed. You may think you've nailed it, and then you get derailed by life. Your purpose will only become clear when you stop struggling and let go, allowing life to flow through you rather than trying to control it. That doesn't mean kicking back with your feet up on your desk. You need to be an active participant to feel, grow, and learn what's right for you.

My life's work now is to inspire peace by educating people about mindful awareness, using a robust practice of martial arts as the working surface. My physical class format doesn't change, but I emphasise turning down the self-talk and allowing some time out from the continual chatter we all know so well. The class becomes a complete body, mind and spirit workout from the inside out.

In writing this book, I've included concepts and ideas that resonate with me. I call them "The Mindset of a Martial Arts Master". But I want to point out that I don't consider myself a master, a guru, or above anyone else in any way. That identity only serves to fire up the ego that I've worked so hard to turn down. Mastery is a fickle concept, and totally personal.

Some of the concepts I present may contradict others, and make it seem as if I've suddenly changed my mind. But they all offer an unbridled truth from deep inside me and provoke thought, contemplation and introspection. I'm not fixated in any way that my truths are the quintessential truths and the only reality. I just allow the ideas to arise within me and express them without attachment to what others may think.

The moves presented in this book are nothing more than concepts. They're not designed to be the perfect defence. I've learned and practised extensively, and allowed the moves to evolve. But they're all built on strong foundations that haven't changed. I was privileged to study with some of the world's greatest Ju Jutsu masters and their senior students for many years. At times the training was brutal, and to really understand the depth of the moves I faced the added challenge of having to learn Japanese.

I first felt the power of real Ju Jitsu in 1991 while training at Katsuyuki Kondo Sensei's Daito Ryu Aiki Ju Jutsu Shimbukan dojo. This was when Kondo Sensei was at his brutal best. The classes were run in the image of the Emperors court. Etiquette was precise and ritualised, and it didn't matter that I wasn't Japanese. He still screamed at me if I got it wrong.

It rattled me at first, but once I understood the language it really challenged my resolve. My ego would push back. He has no right to talk to me that way. I'm already a second dan, blah, blah.

But Sensei didn't care about any of that. He was only concerned with how I reacted to his words. Talk about tough love. He'd yell at me and then walk away without a care in the world, leaving me to stew in my anger. For six months I just wanted to be recognised and told how good I was. But all I got were the same few techniques to do, being yelled at, and toilet cleaning duty.

I was too stubborn to see that my cup was full, and that all they were doing was helping me. They were just hammering down the nail that stood out. And I was the nail.

The delivery may not always be understood by the student, but a great teacher always regards the student's welfare with the utmost importance.

Add to the mix the sheer intensity of the training and the excruciating pain of the techniques, I was deeply challenged at every level—body, mind and spirit.

My thinking always tried to talk me out of going to the dojo. I'd get on the packed train in peak hour at Shinjuku Station, travel 40 minutes to the outer suburb of Shinkoiwa (a very unappealing part of industrial Tokyo), and then walk 20 minutes to the dojo. I walked through the humid hot days of a never-ending summer, the pouring rain of the wet season, and the frozen streets and snow of the bitterly cold winter. But I kept turning up.

Then one day, after six solid months of training, I just let go. I let go of who I thought I was, and the need to be recognised just disappeared. I was fit, my body hardened and strong, my hands, elbows, knees and feet all calloused, and on this day I finally got it.

As part of our warmup we all lined up opposite each other with a thick timber bokken (sword), and with a ferocity of movement struck each other's timber sword (suburi), repeating the cuts anywhere from a hundred to a thousand times. One tiny lapse in concentration and you could be struck down. The great sword master Musashi used a timber sword to defeat his opponents in many challenges.

I was totally engrossed in the sword cuts. I was no longer thinking. I was simply acting. I was deeply aware, and realised that the essence of all activity was to let go completely. And the only way it could happen was to literally shock the body, mind and spirit out of its constant and incessant roundabout of dialogue.

For the next six months I was still having the same thoughts, but my body was on autopilot. I kept training, but before bowing and entering the dojo I parked my ego at the door. I stepped through the dojo entrance, and the instant I felt the hard mats underfoot I was free.

And at the end of the class, after having a holiday from myself, I picked up all the emotional baggage I'd left at the dojo entrance. Except now it felt less intense and had less meaning. It just didn't have the same importance.

The dojo is where the physical warrior meets the spiritual warrior and becomes one.

The dojo is a still and neutral space. It should be clear of clutter, simple and clean. It is a place of developing a deeper understanding of oneself. The dojo is the foundation of the martial arts journey, and a sacred space where one can be themselves. The dojo encourages present awareness.

The techniques all resonate from stillness, and return to stillness. They do not leave a residue within you unless there's an emotion attached to it. It's the instructor's job to keep the students' awareness sharp using the moves of martial arts. In the dojo you will be challenged on every level. The technique starts the moment you enter the dojo, and finishes when you leave. Everything within the dojo is designed to keep you present. This is the way.

Essential elements of martial arts

There's no 'magic' technique that will work in every situation. That's why the foundation and fundamentals of the system need to be well thought out so you can apply the basics effectively as a blueprint, no matter what the situation. Learn them well, and you will enhance the quality of both your martial arts and your life.

1. Awareness/stillness/consciousness.
Being present, focused and able to see situations happening around you. Being aware of your outer space, the space of other people and most importantly your inner space, all working effectively in unison at all times.

2. Balance.
To gain the advantage, the moment you touch you must break your opponent's balance while maintaining your own. There are many ways to break a person's balance, but here are the three I use most often:
1. verbally: yelling, screaming, talking
2. passively: pushing or pulling
3. aggressively: actually striking my opponent.

Learning to break balance should be one of the main focuses of any system you learn, from white belt to black belt. Before any holds, locks or submissions can be determined, balance must be broken. Most people's balance will be well and truly broken after being screamed at or punched in the nose. Your own emotional balance can easily be broken by words. Just do a quick audit on how quickly you become angry or impatient, usually at someone else's expense.

3. Distance.
Maintaining and controlling the distance between you and others. If you can't learn how to control this space, you have no hope of defending yourself effectively. You may overreact and hurt someone unnecessarily, or underreact and put yourself or others in danger.

4. Breath.
Breathing is vital for life. Taking a breath when under stress is critical for clear thinking. It provides a small gap where you can become present, and control

your stress, fear and panic when responding to the situation. By monitoring your opponent's breath, you can choose when to strike—ideally when they're breathing in and you're breathing out.

5. Eyes.
Seeing things for what they are enables you to respond effectively and with clarity. Eyes can be strong, confident and focused, or they can be downcast and afraid. Start by having your eyes up, keeping your shoulders back, and walking with purpose.

6. Structure.
Good martial arts needs a sound structure. It needs to start with the basic concepts that create a foundation strong enough to support the entire system. I see so many schools that don't cover the basics, such as:

» correct stances that enhance taking someone's balance without sacrificing your own

» distance, and how to control the space effectively around you

» awareness, how to practise with it, and why it's so important.

I trained with the founders of a Russian system of martial arts that became quite well known in the early 1990s. It was very popular, and all the trainers I worked out with were excellent. But the system lacked structure. The trainers would say, "Just let your body react". This is okay for experienced martial artists, but the less experienced need basic guidance.

You need form and technique as fundamentals, just as you need letters to learn to read and communicate. But remember: you don't spell the words to talk.

Kata. The application of the essential elements

One of the problems with working techniques in prearranged sequences (known as 'kata') is you can become too familiar with the sequences and make the mistake that you're learning to defend yourself effectively. Your partner can also become familiar with the moves, and may unintentionally help you by deliberately throwing themselves.

That's why having a still, Zen-like demeanour, and being totally in the moment rather than trying to predict what's coming next, is so important in kata work. Kata is a misunderstood concept, and many modern Ju Jitsu schools have taken them out. But they are vital for understanding the basics, and must be included for modern Ju Jitsu to be a valid interpretation of this unique and ancient art of Ju Jutsu.

Kata is also important for breaking balance while maintaining your own. Understanding the importance of judging distance, and being able to effectively enter your opponent's space, deliver the technique and remove yourself without getting injured.

Maintain composure by using your eyes. Ganriki is a sharp penetrating gaze that sees an opponent's intentions and can be used to dominate and control them. At higher levels, reading your opponent's breathing pattern can also be useful in executing the techniques.

Kata is also a useful practise for exploding from zero to 100%, doing the move in its entirety, and then switching off. It allows you to move away feeling unemotional and unattached without carrying any residue.

The last, and probably most important practice missing in most forms of modern Ju Jitsu, is Zanshin. Zanshin usually refers to a mental state where you continue to focus on your opponent and the surrounding environment. I see this as a vital part of learning and executing the technique.

The last thing you want is for the kata to become so stylised that it resembles a dance, devoid of any martial substance. It's easy to think that the moves represent reality, but they only tell part of the story. A violent confrontation is just too random to expect the moves to replicate the kata you practise in the dojo.

The kata is just the signposts for getting the basics right. The basics should be the same for every kata—break balance, monitor the distance, use the breath and eyes, zanshin (awareness).

Some martial arts truths

What drives people to study martial arts is both diverse and interesting. Many want to learn a way of fighting they can use to defend themselves if they need to.

The trick in martial arts is teaching the student to remain open and honest as their skills improve. As they become stronger, fitter and more in control, there's a risk that their new-found power will blind then to the ego's insatiable desire to have more and be more. And this will only inhibit what needs to be an open and honest approach to training.

Here are some more home truths about martial arts.

1. You can learn enough physical skills to defend yourself in an hour. But the mental and emotional skills you need take a lifetime to master. It's how your mind interprets a situation that will dictate whether you'll be able to defend yourself adequately. Many people train in martial arts for years, and still believe they need to learn more to be able to defend themselves. They only address the emotional aspects as they stumble upon them by mistake.

2. The truth in martial arts lies not in the learning of physical moves, but in the observation of the moves as they arise out of stillness.

3. If there's a chance to evoke an opinion or judgement, then your emotional balance has been broken. Most martial artists give up their advantage and clearly indicate their ability simply by the badge on their uniform. Some wear one, while others line their uniforms with them. But they all clearly outline to their opponent exactly what they've studied, and their intention.

4. Your opponent will form an opinion of you in a microsecond based on the way you look, talk, walk, and generally hold yourself. Your ability and excellence as a martial artist will depend on how well you remain neutral under pressure, and your ability to respond clearly to what's needed. Every situation that presents itself is totally neutral.

    All emotions (fear, panic, anger, etc.) rise out of your interpretation of what's happening at that time. Unless you're still, neutral and in control, your reaction/response may not align with what's clearly happening.

    Your ability as a martial artist will be shaped by how well you apply this to daily life. There's no use being a great Sensei in your dojo if you get impatient standing in line, or get angry at the first person who cuts you off in traffic.

5. To be able to respond this way, you need to practise it in all daily activities. It is the martial artist's discipline and ability to bring this 'still awareness' into everyday life that enables them to make martial arts a life choice of peace, and transcend the art of fighting into the art of life.

6. Even the colour and material of your uniform will allow your opponent to make an opinion and formulate a plan to bring you down. While there's attachment and identification to martial arts bling, the ego is clearly involved. Once the bling and dogma are removed, all that's left is martial arts—real martial arts. While there's an attachment to winning or losing, or when winning or losing is the head of the system and not the tail, the system will be no better than a sporting school, void of effective martial art lifestyle.

7. Joining a proper martial arts school is not the same as joining a gym. It takes years to gain the trust of a Sensei. The relationship between Sensei and student grows as the student proves their dedication and commitment to weather the good and the hard times on their martial arts journey. Most people never realise this, and quit before any real learning commences.

8. Martial arts can be a business. In fact, it needs to be a business. Many great teachers can only grow and share their skills if they have a platform to live in the world. Great martial arts leaders offer great service. They have the insight to see the needs of the students and send their message out accordingly. The delivery may not always be understood by the student, but the student's welfare will always be paramount.

9. A great Sensei will take you on a journey. They will walk with you, not in front of or behind you. They will walk beside you and illuminate the path so you can clearly see the way forward. Whether you can fight, get your next belt, become a black belt, win a competition, lose a competition or become a registered trainer, or are learning mixed martial arts (MMA), BJJ, taekwondo or karate is of no consequence.

10. What matters most is your ability to relate to the rest of the world in a way that enables humanity and propagates peace.

One final thing. You often hear Ju Jitsu instructors refer to themselves as 'Professor'. In Australia, referring to yourself as a professor means you have done years of research and study, and have years of hands-on experience at a university. But in Brazil, 'professor' is the term used to indicate 'teacher', much like the Japanese use the term 'Sensei'. Don't be misled by this cultural difference in the term used for 'teacher'.

The modern martial arts school

The following qualities will help make your dojo look and feel special.

Your dojo is a conscious hub. It revolves around awareness that you exist in a space you can control, as well as awareness of others being in spaces they can control, all at the same time without thinking about it.

We start to train ourselves in this open sense of awareness the moment we enter the dojo, and aim to maintain it throughout the class. Every ready stance is a reminder to come back to the present moment and reset ourselves.

The ready stance, a precursor to movement, is just a metaphor. As you do it, become still and emotionally aware of what you're going through and what's happening. Your fight or flight is highly tuned, and you must decide. But first you need to be able to see the choices.

That may mean raising your open hands as you would in a fighting stance. But you do not close your fists. You want to appear neutral, not aggressive or angry. Having your hands up will ensure your safety in a fiery, out of control situation. If you're aware of your choices, you can move quickly with clarity and purpose once you make your decision.

After spending years battling the Gauls in what is now greater Europe, Julius Caesar amassed a huge and powerful army. At Rome the senate, fuelled by Cicero and other Roman power brokers, feared Caesar would march on with his army and take control of Rome. So even after his great victory over Gaul for Rome, Caesar was declared an outlaw.

This infuriated Caesar, and so he set off for Rome with his army.

The point of no return for Caesar was the Rubicon River. Once he crossed it, he was certain a war with Rome would follow.

In combat, you must decide whether you will cross your own Rubicon. That is, take a risk and cross the distance between you and your opponent and stay in range while you unleash your techniques. This is what I call 'working in the pocket'.

I've studied an ancient Hindu Vedantic tradition. Within the age-old teachings are many timeless gems that are still very relevant today. The Bhagavat Gita and the Upanishads are like the Hindu bible, and are packed with many wise lessons. I like to use some of those lessons in the foundation study of Northstar Ju Jitsu.

I often gently refer to the mahaguna in my teachings as well. These are three states of consciousness—Rajas, Tamas and Sattwa.

- » Rajas is fiery, red, aggressive, charged up, competitive and stressful, and reflects the flow of consciousness..

- » Tamas is dark, heavy, dull, black and depressed, and absorbs the flow of consciousness.

- » Sattwa is light, clean, airy, white and meditative, and conducts the flow of consciousness.

None of them is superior to the others. They're just a nice way to explain how you're feeling. In fact, we can quickly and easily rotate between them as much as we change our mood.

All three are present in my dojo, constantly rotating. For the best mindful experience, the dojo needs to be Sattwa at the beginning of class so people can learn and grow in their own way at their own pace.

It starts as a clean, still and neutral space, with no eating or loud talking allowed. During the class, the dojo will go through Tamas and Rajas. And then at the end of the class we finish with some softer techniques to bring us back down and leave the dojo and ourselves in Sattwa. All clutter and bags are removed or packed away. The dojo is cleaned, the pads are straightened, and any rubbish on the shelves is removed

It is returned to its original state.

When they all work together in unison, people who visit will feel the special quality of the space. They may not be able to put their finger on what it is about the dojo. It happens on a subliminal level beyond their everyday thought. They just feel it in their body, mind and spirit.

Awareness

To understand awareness and start including it in your life is one of the greatest keys to living a fulfilling life. Most people live in a state of constant reaction to the never-ending stream of seemingly benign events, wondering why they're suffering and so unhappy. On an uncontrolled impulse anger is just a breath away, and before they know it they've crossed the line and know their life will never be the same.

What's sad is that all of this can be avoided.

The problem is these people are their anger, impatience and violence. And in a perverse way they're comfortable with that. They take the coward's approach, preferring to live their lives in silent suffering at the expense of those closest to them. And they'll never change, because the die has been cast.

The good news is that by using some simple techniques you can become aware of this pattern of behaviour and change it, rather than suffering needlessly. Instead of saying "This is just who I am, and I'll never change", you'll be able to see the pattern unfolding and choose to not take it on. Eventually you'll learn to distance yourself from these habitual patterns that have been a part of your life for so long.

In effect, you'll be creating change from the inside out.

You're not trying to eradicate years of conditioning. Instead you're building your awareness muscle so you can decide whether to buy into the behaviour or watch it rise and then disappear, leaving you calm and in control.

This is where real mastery happens in martial arts. It's the true meaning of developing mind and spirit. Unfortunately, most martial artists don't understand this.

Awareness enables choice. With practice you'll be able to choose how you respond in every interaction. But without that awareness the choice will be made for you through habit. An angry person isn't angry out of choice. They're angry because they habitually react in the same way to the same thing time and time again.

Awareness, stillness and consciousness are all the same thing.

The first step in martial arts is to become aware that you exist, and that there is a space around you. This may sound pretty obvious, but a huge proportion of the population are completely unaware of their own existence. They may say "But I'm alive, aren't I?" They get so caught up in their own head that they forget they have a body.

The second step is to control that space around you by monitoring it and choosing who enters it. Martial arts is never about fighting. It's about deflecting any intrusion into your personal space. Knowing this space exists puts you ahead of anyone who doesn't, which seems to be most of the population. You can simply move away the instant someone enters your space, as you've already recognised the action by being aware.

If you're aware of that space around you, and the fact you can control it, then being aware of other people and the space around them is the next step. If you know you have a space around you that you can monitor, you should be able to sense when you're infringing on someone else's.

If you know this, you need to acknowledge it. You can march into someone else's space, or you can take control by practising the forgotten art of courtesy. Chances are the other person won't even be aware that you've entered their space. As you say, "Excuse me", they won't even realise you're talking to them.

The lesson in martial arts is being aware these spaces exist, and then learning to harness the power that comes with entering and controlling them. Once you can control these zones of awareness, you will have a completely different perspective on life.

If I told you, "You are not your thoughts", you'd probably think I'm a raving lunatic. So let's keep this simple. Real freedom comes when you're totally immersed in what you're doing and not thinking about the past or future.

When you're listening to that inspiring piece of music, or surfing, or playing your favourite sport, you are totally indulged in the moment. You're not thinking about yesterday or tomorrow. You're free from all ego, and you simply exist.

But here's the thing. The moment you start thinking about being present, you are not.

Practice being present by simply listening without judgement, seeing without judgement, tasting without judgement and being without judgement.

Balance

In Ju Jitsu, the key to maintaining good form, executing technique correctly and surviving under pressure is to maintain your own balance as you work to take the balance of your opponent. On a physical level, you maintain your balance by not overextending, not pushing too hard, and applying just enough power to achieve the desired outcome.

If you find yourself overextending, it means you haven't judged the distance between you and your target well enough. You need to learn not to push too hard and to apply just enough power so you can judge the amount you need by feel.

You learn and master the correct technique in class by maintaining and constantly adjusting your form. First you practise without focus mitts or strike shields, and then you start applying strong power against them. This is a great way to ensure you maintain your good form and balance. If you strike the pad incorrectly, or don't get your distance correct, you'll quickly overbalance and lose your advantage.

A common problem students have with pad work is trying too hard with too much power. Power is good, but power and good timing is better. A student can be powerful and look quite strong, but if their timing is off it can significantly reduce the impact of their strike.

Concentrate on form and good technique during the first part of the class without the pads, and then maintain that form while striking the pads (e.g. keep your hands up and elbows in, recoil your leg after striking when you're kicking). This will improve your balance, and the effectiveness of your martial arts training.

The next step is to maintain your balance while training with a partner, such as with two-man kata and sparring. The basics still apply, except now you're under extra pressure because someone is hitting back. So it becomes a game of balance where the odds are a little less in your favour.

In South Korea I found a National Hapkido Association that had literally been turned into a dance. How funny.

Why all the different ways to spell Ju Jutsu?

Yes, it can be confusing. But they all mean the same thing.

'Ju Jutsu' is translated from the Chinese characters used in the Japanese language. 'Ju' can be translated to mean 'tender, weakness, gentleness, softness', while 'Jutsu' can be translated to mean 'art, technique, skill, means, trick, resources'. (There are different interpretations in the translation.)

While 'Ju Jutsu' is the more traditional translation, I tend to use 'Ju Jitsu' simply because it's easier to say.

All you need to remember is they both refer to the same form of martial art, and not two different ones.

There's confusion among many students of Brazilian Jiu Jitsu. The misguided belief is that BJJ is the one and only original form of Ju Jitsu. The truth is that BJJ is a hybririd of Judo. Judo was created from traditional Japanese Ju Jutsu.

What's missing from modern Ju Jitsu?

Modern Ju Jitsu is suffering from a huge void. The techniques, a convenient mixture of judo and karate, use power and brute force to gain control and force a submission. Balance generally isn't broken, and there's no use or understanding of 'Ju' or 'aiki' to initially put your opponent in pain, take control, then break or dislocate the limb.

Is learning a traditional martial art good for self-defence?

Fighting has been an innate part of humanity since life on earth began. Humans have fought in the past, they're fighting now, and unless there's a major shift in human consciousness they'll continue to fight.

In that time we've had many styles of fighting that have been lost to history. The might of the Roman Centurion was a fighting machine. The gladiators learned their own craft. And the Saxon way of the broadsword and shield was embraced by the Vikings and the Danes.

But the Japanese were different. They were a feudal nation. Clans fought with each other for hundreds of years, and the samurai caste remained until the end of the 1900s. It took their loss in World War II to force them into lasting peace.

So how did the Japanese retain the historical knowledge of their fighting skills when so many others were lost?

The Japanese traditional martial arts taught sword fighting, archery, spears and Ju Jutsu under the same roof called a Ryu. These Ryu were then passed on from headmaster to son. And some of them made it to the 20th century, although they changed a little bit along the way. (One of the most famous Ryu is the renowned Katori Shinto Ryu.)

At the beginning of the 20th century, when the samurai caste was finally outlawed, many of these Ryu closed their doors, downsized or went underground. After World War II, Americans occupied Japan and most martial arts were banned.

This is when Ju Jitsu flourished in its new version called Judo and Aiki Ju Jitsu and went on to become Aikido. Both reflected a change in feudal techniques and became ways of peace.

Many of the Ryu that survived re-emerged years later but nothing like they once were. Most teach only one aspect, such as Ju Jitsu or sword. The young Japanese simply aren't interested in maintaining these ancient, traditional relics. In fact, the only way most will survive is by spreading their art worldwide, as it's the non-Japanese who have the interest.

If you find a good martial arts instructor who teaches one of these traditional martial arts, consider yourself lucky. But don't be fooled into thinking you're learning usable self-defence. As I've always said, you need to learn the old to understand the new. For example, I started out learning Taekwondo. But at the same time I was filling in some of the gaps with boxing and kick boxing. After that I learned the traditional Ju Jutsu that evolved into judo, and so on.

The traditional martial arts systems are good for solid basics, and go well if you train in a modern martial art as well. Again, use the old to understand the new. I trained with the Tenjin Shin Yo Ryu (Tenjin evolved into modern judo) on Wednesdays nights and Saturday mornings, and modern judo on Monday and Thursday nights.

When you are present in action you are totally neutral. No feelings of anger or other emotions intrude. You are now very dangerous, as you have absolutely no feelings towards your opponent or their wellbeing.

Judo and Ju Jitsu

Both of these fighting systems are great forms of martial arts. And yes, they are related.

The traditional martial arts of Ju Jutsu evolved in Japan along two main lines. The empty hand techniques were designed and used on the battlefields to supplement the use of weapons rather than being the focus. Martial arts systems such as yawara and tai-jutsu were specifically used by soldiers and other forms of Ju Jutsu were created by law enforcement for maintaining law and order.

These forms of Ju Jutsu were very effective. But the old ways of the sword no longer had a place in a developing Japan.

One of the most famous forms of Ju Jutsu was founded by Iso Maetomon. He studied both Muso Ryu and Shin no Shinto Ryu, and founded Tenjin Shin-yo Ryu. Maetomon's emphasis was on empty hand (no weapons) techniques, although he still maintained the fighting skills, realism and effectiveness of the old Ju Jutsu schools. Atemi—kicks, fists, elbows and knees—were a specialty of the exponents of Tenjin Shin-yo Ryu. He attracted many students to his dojo, but most were not military men. (They used the term 'commoner'.)

By the end of the Edo period (1603–1868) and the beginning of the Meiji period more than 700 schools were using Ju Jutsu techniques, mostly without weapons. These styles evolved to become aesthetic in nature, and almost completely devoid of martial arts effectiveness.

Jigaro Kano (the founder of modern Judo) entered the Tenjin shin-yo school in 1877. His teacher was the headmaster Hachinosuke, who was taught by founder Maetomon. The training was quite severe, and unlike many other forms of martial arts at the time because the striking training was still very effective. On the death of his teacher, Kano joined the Kito Ryu in 1881.

This school also lacked martial fibre, focusing on nage waza (throwing techniques). Ju Jutsu was slowly disappearing as Japan tried to establish its identity in a rapidly developing world. The few remaining experts struggled to gain students and recognition.

Kano resolved to re-establish Ju Jutsu as a legitimate national pastime worthy of the Meiji era and its ancient reputation.

In 1882, Kano synthesized all his knowledge, including what he learned from the Tenjin Shin-yo Ryu and Kito Ryu, into what he called Kodokan Judo. He then taught it to nine students at the Eisho-ji temple in Tokyo. Using martial arts as a way to improve the body, mind and spirit really appealed to Kano.

At the time Ju Jutsu had many moves that were quite violent (participants were injured regularly), and was considered a rough and somewhat uncouth form of training.

Kano didn't want to be aligned the with Ju Jutsu name.

In 1886 Kano accepted the now famous challenge from the Yoshin Ryu Ju Jutsu, organised by the Tokyo Police. Fifteen fighters from each school were pitted against each other. The judo team won all but two bouts, and the Yoshin Ryu team was decimated by the Kodokan's Saigo Shiro's masterful use of Yama Arashi.

What isn't well known is that Yama Arashi was a Daito Ryu Aiki Ju Jutsu technique he had learned previously.

Kano was emphatic about including kata (pre-arranged fighting moves) in all structures of training. He believed it not only improved the physical conditioning of the body but also stimulated intellectual development. Kano considered the personal character of all his students to be the real test of their values, and required them to live their lives in a dignified manner.

Kano's own outstanding example inspired all who came to the Kodokan. Judo went on to become an international and Olympic sport that set the wheels in motion from its humble beginning to an incredible movement known as modern martial arts.

Going further, Brazilian Ju Jitsu (BJJ) can trace its history back to Jigaro Kano at the time judo was transitioning into a martial art and sport. Top Brazilian grapplers pitted their skills against the best Japanese judo exponents, paving the way for BJJ to be recognised as a martial art and sport worldwide.

The martial artist, the street fighter and the MMA fighter?

The age-old question of what's the toughest, most superior way of fighting isn't as clean cut as it seems. And trying to answer it in broad terms would be a gross injustice to all forms of combat.

The ignorant may dismiss martial artists, saying they hide behind their secret techniques. They may also be seen as high and mighty in their stand that deadly techniques be removed from sports competition, thereby giving them the air of 'lethal weapon' without ever having to prove themselves.

But anyone who says martial artists can't hold their own obviously hasn't stepped into a proper martial arts dojo and asked to spar.

Mixed martial arts (MMA) and Ultimate Fighting Challenge (UFC) competitions may have led to a resurgence of the now defunct argument that non-contact karateka and other forms of traditional martial arts aren't worthy of their reputation. But judging an entire heritage and tradition on a handful of inexperienced fighters is for people who still argue that "My dad is bigger than your dad" and have never gotten over it.

Many great fighters are also martial artists. Some of my toughest sparring matches have been against traditional karate and taekwondo stylists—fast, efficient, brutal, and well versed in all aspects of fighting. Back in the late '80s there was a league of martial artists who competed in teams every three weeks in New South Wales, Victoria and Queensland. It was a lot of fun, and all the great martial arts competitors got into the spirit of the competition.

Saturday afternoon was an open sparring class, which wasn't a place for the faint-hearted. You knew you'd have to fight, and that it would be a case of 'hurt or be hurt'. Some days there were 40–50 black belts from all styles, and I respected them all. They were excellent martial artists, excellent fighters and excellent men. No quarter was ever asked for—or ever given.

In contrast, the average street fighter is a thug who'll king-hit you when you look the other way. Yes, I understand there are no rules on the street. But street fighters (if they still exist) are usually undisciplined, out-of-control brawlers who will run the moment they're on the losing side of a scrap.

Fighting and sparring other highly trained black belts is a very dangerous pastime. One false slip or overextension and you can be badly hurt, knocked out or even killed. When you train and spar this way you're up against incredibly skilled exponents with years of training, competition and security work experience.

You can enter an MMA, boxing or kickboxing fight after specialised training, often with only a few weeks' experience. Take nothing away from them. They're tough, courageous people. But they're still very much beginners.

Twenty years ago, Brazilian Jiu Jitsu master Rorian Gracie came up with the idea to test his students' skills against other martial arts exponents in a way that had never been seen before. The fights took place in a specially designed octagon, complete with fencing that could only be climbed over. This 'no escape"'mentality, combined with limited rules that allowed most hand and feet strikes including elbows and knees, judo, wrestling and ju jitsu throws and groundwork, was the birth of what's now known as the Ultimate Fighting Challenge (UFC).

The UFC quickly grew in popularity worldwide. And the UFC fighters had to adapt just as quickly. They soon learned that a weakness in any of the three ranges of fighting—standing (punching and kicking) throwing or groundwork—would immediately be exposed, threatening a potential loss.

So the trainers, contestants and training partners set out to fill the gaps in their training regime, usually by cross-training in other styles and systems that offered immediate results. And from this mix of styles a hybrid system of training was developed called Mixed Martial Arts (MMA).

This style of training takes only the best techniques that enhance the chances of winning the fight or competition. Most martial arts training is a combination of traditional systems that have evolved into a new hybrid. Judo and Aikido are great examples of this.

MMA is a tough sport, and I respect anyone who has the courage to step into the ring. It's also great for fitness and conditioning.

MMA/UFC is a by-product of martial arts, so let's not forget where it came from. UFC competitors undoubtedly fight in a realm that's closest to reality (compared to other forms of martial arts competition, boxing, etc.) They're hardened athletes, and train to hit and hurt. And to the untrained eye (and those with limited experience in martial arts), they would appear to be the best martial arts has to offer. But thankfully the only similarity they have to real martial arts is that some of the techniques look similar, just as some of the hand techniques of karate look similar to boxing.

The term 'martial art' really has no place in an arena such as the UFC. Martial arts has a depth to it that takes the exponent on a journey far beyond the physical. The need to fight and prove oneself is just one of the skins the martial artist sheds on the way to realising what the training is for—confrontation of self, your toughest adversary.

Most martial artists only ever get as far as fighting and learning to defend their physical body. When they get tired they retire and quit like any other sportsman. Very few move past the physical and attempt to gain mastery of self.

This is in no way a criticism of this new way of fighting. But it's important to remember that MMA/UFC is a spinoff of martial arts (just as kickboxing and Taebo were in the '90s) rather than an evolution of it.

Kickboxing is also a spinoff of martial arts. In fact, the stalwarts of modern kickboxing—Bill Wallace, Joe Lewis and Benny the Jet—were all traditional karate stylists before they pioneered kickboxing.

There are great and not-so-great fighters in all areas of combat. Which style is best? It really comes down to the individual and their ability to tap into their killer instinct.

A Scottish man I worked with many years ago rolled onto Central station with a tummy full of beer and was set upon by five thugs. He turned and fought with every ounce of power, and ended up putting three of them in hospital. It was the first fight he'd ever been in, and hadn't had a day's training in his life.

One night I worked on the door with a new doorman who was an "expert in Ninjutsu", full of bravado and stories of his latest fighting conquests. A bit of a push and shove on the door escalated very quickly, and the last I saw of the Ninja was him copping a forearm to the side of the head because he didn't even know the basics of fighting: "Keep your hands up, son".

So, there are no hard and fast rules. We all have the ability to fight, but how far you can push someone before they lash out is totally up to the individual and their own personal evolution.

The style doesn't make the man. The man makes the style.

Karate

Karate is probably the most well-known of all the martial arts, and enjoyed by adults and children of all ages.

Karate was born in the islands of Okinawa, and later developed and refined in Japan. The generic word 'karate' eventually spread throughout the world to represent all oriental martial arts.

While all karate fighting systems use the hands, feet, elbows and knees as weapons, different styles and classes have developed since its inception. One of the oldest styles is Shotokan karate. Based on ancient principles, it's probably the most famous and well known of the karate schools. Goju Ryu is another very famous style of Karate.

Most karate schools have kata (set patterns), self-defence and sparring in the syllabus, and use the belt system—starting at white and working towards black—for grading students.

Some compete in non-contact competitions, while others such as Kyokushin karate focus on full contact.

Karate will give you great basics and good self-defence skills. The training is traditional, and commonly uses Japanese terminology. The classes are also quite physical, making fitness and conditioning a great by-product of the training.

From the traditions of karate, Tatsuo Yamada became interested in the full-contact applications of karate after seeing Thais perform Muay Thai boxing in the ring. The main moves of kickboxing can be traced back to the original full-contact karate styles such as kyokushin. In the beginning kickboxing allowed head butts and throws, clearly separating it from Thai boxing, but these allowances were removed as the rules evolved.

The first kickboxing association was formed in 1966 by Japanese Osamu Noguchi, and the first kickboxing event was held in Japan in 1966. In the USA, karate was modified into full-contact ring fights as early as the mid-60s. But it wasn't until the mid-70s that proper sanctioned organisations were formed to cope with the new popular sport of kickboxing. It has now spread worldwide, evolving into many different associations and variations on the rules.

Kickboxing is a great form of martial arts in its own right. It has modernised the traditional side of the art, and transformed karate into a simple yet robust and effective form of sport fighting that can also be used for self-defence.

However, traditionalists may contend that it doesn't resemble a martial art as it has no etiquette or connection to a lineage. And in a way that's true.

Kickboxing training has some terrific by-products, such as weight loss and conditioning. As fighters need to be in great shape, the training includes drills, bag work, skipping and sparring. Many gyms around the world now include white-collar kickboxing for men and women so they can enjoy the robust training without the contact.

Many personal trainers can be seen in parks training clients on the pads, and the fitness industry recognises many of the kickboxing accreditation programs.

Sport martial arts vs. martial arts

Sport has its place in martial arts. But have too much of it and the martial art loses its identity.

The Ju Jutsu of old wasn't concerned with sport. In fact, it went the other way. The techniques focused on dislocating and breaking joints, strangling and throwing. Designed to maim or kill, it was primarily used in matters of life and death.

The modern arts of judo and Brazilian Ju Jitsu, along with some of the modern Ju Jitsu schools, have strong sporting components while still retaining the values of traditional martial arts.

It's easy to put martial arts in the 'sports' category and leave it there. But getting lost in winning the game signals the demise of martial arts. Sport has its place in martial arts, but it needs to be the tail and not the head. I run two competitions a year, and they're great fun and really good for the students.

Unfortunately, many instructors lean towards competition because they have nowhere else to go. Competing and winning fuels and powers up the ego, but this won't suit all your students and doesn't bring out the best in everyone.

Winning can be the goal of any competition. But losing can also be a great lesson. Most of the world's top sports people have lost far more than they've won. Losing is healthy when it creates a willingness to learn more with determination and resilience, and to overcome the odds and try harder.

On the surface there's nothing wrong with a bit of healthy martial arts competition. I competed in many of them, and always used them to confront my own limitations and seek out personal growth.

The problem is that for many martial arts, competing is their primary purpose. This leads the public, who really don't know the difference, to believe martial arts is just another sport. There's a winner and a loser, and an ancient tradition becomes nothing more than a game.

Unfortunately, this is the reality of modern martial arts. With the next Olympic Games in Tokyo, Japanese karate is striving to become an Olympic sport and take its place beside judo and taekwondo, which have already lost their identity in the rush to get Olympic recognition.

We're constantly being told to get ahead, pass the exam, be someone, be something. Martial arts needs to be a safe haven where there's no competition. It needs to be a place where everyone is recognised for their uniqueness and encouraged accordingly—especially when they're children.

Behind the desire to win is the ego's insatiable appetite for recognition. In martial arts, the various associations are blinded by the glory of their students. Their studios are stuffed with medals and plastic trophies, and made to look like the shrines built to honour great warriors. It's not their fault. They simply haven't been taught do act in any other way.

Judo was never meant to a standalone sport. But like taekwondo it became an Olympic sport because it had no other way to develop.

Sparring

Most people who enter a martial arts studio participate in sparring. This can be daunting for many people as it means stepping way out of their comfort zone. Choosing to stand in front of another person with your hands up, ready to punch and kick in free and random movement, can be a huge decision for men and women of all ages.

Sparring can range from strict non-contact to a fight for survival. I totally get people being nervous about sparring for the first time because if it's not facilitated professionally it can easily get out of hand.

I include some kind of free movement in every class I teach. It keeps it real. But the sparring I teach is specifically designed to be robust but safe. And every student is closely monitored, regardless of their level or experience.

Having spent many years doing many kinds of sparring, I often think about the value of doing it. To be considered self-defence it needs to be done in a way that resembles a real fight. But that can lead to frequent and sometimes nasty injuries.

Sparring is great fun, and a perfect way to challenge the edges of your comfort zone. ultimately it's a sensitivity drill that can really add to your overall martial arts experience.

Starting from the ground up, you're trying to feel the energetic movements—not the power of your partner. Feeling the energetic movements is very subtle, and you need to be relaxed. By learning to feel, you can respond well before you feel their strength and power.

When you're rolling in close proximity with someone, you get better at feeling their energy. The next step is to stand and grapple, and see if you can still relax and feel the same energy. Then you slowly move apart to create a short distance, which is where it can get a little crazy. Just see if you can stay in touch with the energetic field of your partner as you enter the standing sparring range.

This is not a 'hocus pocus' circus trick, like the 'ki' masters who can seemingly repel any attack by their students, and then stupidly agree to take on a fighter who then beats them up.

This exercise simply helps you create a deeper awareness of yourself and your surroundings a little bit at a time.

Drawing your sword

When the sword is drawn, you have to cut. So if you're not prepared to go all the way, keep the sword firmly in the scabbard.

I liken raising your fists to drawing your sword. If you raise your fists, you'd better be willing to go all the way. If you're not, then you should just walk on.

Some people just aren't aware, and bring their the sword out (partly or entirely) at the slightest provocation. It could be as innocuous as honking their horn to warn someone or asking their neighbour to turn down the music. But now it's too late, and they find themselves in a situation they can no longer control.

There is a way to do this. And it usually involves not leading with your right cross.

Mastery is seeing the desire to respond with anger or aggression as it rises, pausing for one breath, and then watching it fade. Only in this action do you have choice.

Authentic Ju Jitsu. The Japanese art of self-defence

Traditional and modern systems of Ju Jitsu teach both throwing and ground moves from the beginning of the student's journey.

But the Northstar Ju Jitsu style is a little different. Though greatly influenced by traditional Japanese Ju Jitsu, my students don't learn how to throw until they've been training for at least six months. Instead, they learn a comprehensive syllabus of striking techniques so they can break balance as an immediate strike without getting tangled up trying to lock up, throw or go to ground.

This gives them a base level of being able to defend themselves while they remain standing. And it becomes a strong foundation they can refer to whenever the more advanced techniques don't work.

From this grounded and stable base, they can add throws, locks and other moves once balance is broken. And as they continue to train and improve, they learn to interweave their strikes with movement and techniques that complete the application of Ju Jitsu moves.

Most modern Ju Jitsu systems I've observed are hybrids of judo, which was the first modern interpretation of traditional Ju Jutsu. I'm not saying they're not effective, but most put the cart before the horse by only including striking to break balance as an afterthought.

Simple ways to living an evolved martial art life

I've included the following points to help you bring some of the concepts in this book into your life.

1. **When someone pushes, move a side and let them pass.** This takes strength of mind, as your previous action would be to resist, make a point, or have a compulsive need to give your opinion. Just try to be still and quiet every now and then and see what happens.

2. **Become aware of the space between you and others.**
   Being aware of that space means you can control it. And once you know about this space, you instantly become aware of how you move in others' space. For the next couple of weeks, when the overpowering need to get your stuff done arises, think about how you may be intruding on other people's spaces.

3. **Smile in conflict.**
   Quite often when we're training, pushing, shoving, sparring and practicing self-defence, there is a real buzz in the dojo. There's talking and even laughing, and people are really connecting. Strange, isn't it? When you go about your daily routines, try to connect with the same lightness. Give life a lighter, simpler touch, and try not to take yourself too seriously.

4. **Practice Determination**
   Believe you can succeed and go beyond your perceived barriers, regardless of your current situation. Use the small wins in life to prepare you for the big challenges. Sometimes when you're in the depths of despair and depression, a tiny flicker of hope is enough to help you put one foot in front of the other. Challenge yourself constantly by facing your fears.

5. **Acknowledge the support and caring of others by offering gratitude.** Generosity of spirit strengthens your ability to forgive, and opens your heart to receive. "What's in it for me?" has no place here.

6. **Keep your own counsel.**
    Own your thoughts, actions, plans and dreams. Only you know what they mean to you. If you're constantly swayed by the crowd, surprise yourself and others by starting to believe that your own uniqueness is special and worthy. This is how leadership is developed.

7. **Accept change.**
    In fighting you have to adapt and move very quickly. The instant you get set in your ways you get hit. This is a great metaphor for living. If you are too set into believing your reality will never change, when it does change, there can be incredible suffering.

8. **Be fluid and supple, and friendly with life.** Decide that from this moment on you will never be less than friendly towards yourself.

Practice these simple life skills and see what happens.

Breakfalls

Ever watched a rugby match?

Sometimes it can take 3–5 players to bring their opponent to the ground. It's not easy to take someone down who really wants to stay on their feet.

This series shows the most basic breakfall. I believe breakfalls were designed solely to be able to take a throw in the dojo. This form of breakfall shouldn't be used on hard or unpadded surfaces.

The only real value of this kind of breakfall outside of the dojo is that it teaches you how to protect the head and land in the best position. In reality when you breakfall you should use your entire body.

In the Northstar Ju Jitsu syllabus, we don't put a great deal of emphasis on learning to breakfall for the first couple of belts. I don't want you to get comfortable being taken onto the ground. I want you to be able to fight to remain standing and use your strikes to break your opponent's balance.

You can do this initially from kneeling, and then standing when you're comfortable.

1. Bring your right hand up to your left ear.
2. Swing your right leg forward.
3. Collapse your left leg, going onto the ground on your side. At the same time, strike the mat with your right hand palm down at an angle of about 30 degrees from your body.

Keep your head and neck off the ground.

Protect your groin with your left hand.

Rear Collar Grab

Major influence: Daito Ryu Aiki Ju Jutsu

"The instant that you are touched, you must unbalance your opponent."

What is a true master?

Is there an overriding definition of mastery?

A true master looks at improving all aspects of their life. Mastery in any field doesn't mean the journey has ended. While mastery implies a level of excellence, there is always more to learn, to study and to experience.

I've learned that true masters are honest in their desire and ability to pass on their knowledge, and do so with goodwill. The information isn't kept secret. Instead, it's open and shared with abundance.

1. Your opponent grabs your rear collar. It's time to touch and unbalance. You need to act quickly as you can easily be pulled back and down.

2. Step forward with your right leg, slightly pulling your opponent forward and off balance. Turn on the spot, block and strike with a closed fist that comes up outside of your opponent's visual field, striking under the chin.

3. Again, break your opponent's balance. Being hit is painful, and not something you can get used to—especially being hit underneath the jaw.

6. Pivoting on your left leg, making a hole for your opponent to fall into.

7. Draw your opponent onto their stomach. Get down on your knees keeping your opponent's arm in tight.

  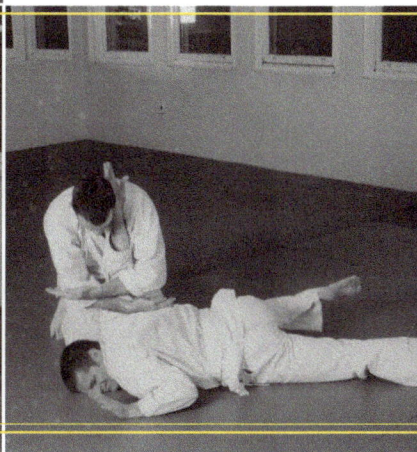

4. This style of striking is really effective because your opponent will only know they have been hit when they feel the pain, they won't see or hear it coming.

5. If their arm is still in range, cup their shoulder or elbow tightly with both hands and step back with your right leg.

8. Turn from their shoulder, causing pain.

If you continue with this submission you may dislocate their arm.

Single Neck Grab

Main influence: Northstar Ju Jitsu

"Controlling the distance between you and your opponent is vital for effective self-defence."

Mastery doesn't mean perfection. It means constantly learning, experiencing and growing. It doesn't mean enlightenment. It means sharing, openness and abundance.

1. Your opponent grabs your neck with one hand and squeezes.

2. This is a very aggressive attack. You need to respond quickly before the strike comes.

   Turn your head and shoulders inward, creating a gap between your neck and your opponent's hand. You may also need to move your body back to loosen the grip. Bring your outside hand over your opponent's arm that's grabbing your neck.

   Grab the thumb with your thumb and the closest finger to their thumb.

3. Putting pressure on their thumb, draw it over their shoulder and away from you, pivoting on their thumb, making sure you apply pain.

   Use your other hand to control their elbow.

4. Continuing the motion over the shoulder, take your opponent down, without leaning over continue the pressure on the thumb and hand and/or apply a wrist lock.

Basic Grabs

Main influence: Tenjin Shinyo Ju Jutsu

Learning the traditional martial arts has its place, but is limited in modern combat effectiveness. Learn the old and then the new. Or even better, learn the updated version of the old.

Your opponent has entered your space and taken your wrist. This situation can be difficult to interpret correctly. How much force should you use?

From my experience, other forms of martial arts have only an 'On' switch, and use full force immediately. In some situations this may be the appropriate response. But what if the other person is simply trying to get your attention?

That's why I believe it's very important to teach what I call "passive defence." This is a first line of action that clearly states your needs and intentions, and removes yourself by creating distance from your opponent.

And it's done without hurting anyone and needlessly inflaming the situation.

Learning effective passive defence gives you the ability to make a choice. You can quickly escalate the situation to "aggressive defence", or use all your basic striking to take control.

For these techniques to be fully effective, you need to use them before your opponent gets a good grip. And to do that you need to have a finely tuned sense of awareness and move quickly. These moves are often used in judo (a direct descendant of Tenjin Shinyo Ryu) where no striking is allowed.

Wrist grab

1. Create a firm base, with you legs shoulder-width apart and one foot slightly in front of the other. Extend the fingers of your hand being clasped. Rest your other hand on your upper thigh, ready to take action. Maintain eye contact, and don't forget to breathe.
2. Step back with the leg on the side not being clasped. At the same time, take your hand in a direct line so the thumb of your clasped hand goes to your ear. This movement will remove your hand from your opponent's grip by attacking the weak spot between their thumb and index finger. It's important to have a long arc and fullness of movement.

Double wrist grab

1. Your opponent grabs both of your wrists. Step back and create some distance while extending the fingers of both of your hands. Relax your shoulders, maintain eye contact, and breathe.
2. Bring both of your arms up, taking your opponent's balance.
3. Continue the motion upward in a long movement so your thumbs go to your ears. This movement attacks your opponent's weak spots between their thumb and index finger.

Single lapel grab

You need to act quickly with this attack. Your opponent has made their intention very clear. Grabbing you in this manner is a very aggressive move. But if you move quickly enough you can still remove yourself without striking and escalating the situation.

1. Move your leg back to a semi-fighting stance—left leg forward, right leg back, and weight evenly distributed on both legs. Place your right hand directly under the hand grabbing you with your thumb up and your little finger down. Rest and ready your left hand on your left thigh.
2. Bring your right hand up while lifting your elbow, and put pressure on the weak spot—your opponent's little finger.
3. Keep drawing your hand back (step back further if you need to) and break the grip of your opponent.

Double lapel grab

Anyone who grabs you in this way has seriously bad intentions. Your ability to respond to this using passive defence will test your skill as a serious martial artist.

1. As with the single hand grab, place your right hand tightly under and up against your opponent's left hand. Have your legs in a semi-fighting stance, relaxed and balanced, and your left hand on your left thigh.
2. Raise your right hand and lift your elbow, cutting at the grip of your opponent and their little finger in particular. At the same time, bring up your left hand so it's vertical to the ground. With your forearm and hand, cut and put pressure on your opponent's wrists.
3. Put the movements of your left and right arms together. Lift your left arm and cut with your right arm to release the grip of your attacker.

Bear Hug. Arms Free

Main Influence: Northstar Ju Jitsu

The moment you react you are drawing your sword. And when you draw your sword, you'd better be prepared to go all the way. Stop, breathe, become present, and respond with knowledge of what's happening now and not what you've experienced in the past.

The term 'martial art' is no longer relevant. It was always a loose term to describe an unorganised splintered group of egomaniacs interested only in promoting themselves for their own needs. They head uselessly into sport or an overemphasis on aesthetics simply because they have nowhere else to go. Why? Because no-one has shown them.

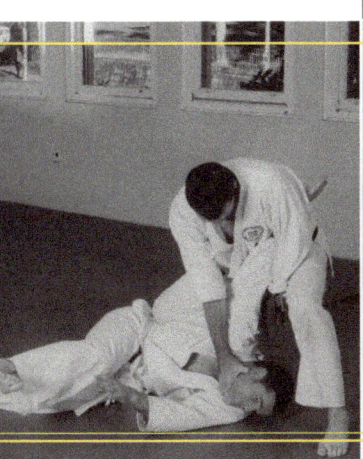

1. Your opponent steps in to grab you around the waist. Depending on the level of aggression, control the distance by either stepping in and intercepting or stepping back so they can't get a firm hold.

2. From a firm and stable base, place your left hand on your opponent's lower back to stop the other from moving back. Then strike with a right elbow or forearm, continuing to break balance.

3. Transfer your right hand to their left lapel or, for a more effective defence, cup your hand under their chin. Keep a strong left hand on their lower back.

4. Sweep out their left leg with your right leg while pushing their chin, slamming your opponent into the ground.

5. With your right knee, pin your opponent to the ground. Make sure your weight is spread evenly across both of your legs. Maintain a loose hold of their arm. Push your thumb into the pressure point just behind their ear.

6. Bring your right arm up as high as it can go and, like a pile driver, strike down hard.

Bear Hug. Pinned

Main Influence: Northstar Ju Jitsu

Aiki. Your opponent needs to feel you before they see or hear you. You need to be dealing with the action, not playing catch-up by reacting. By then it's too late.

You can defend yourself from this attack in a number of ways. Your opponent may squeeze you, then try to lift you up. It's important to immediately try and break the grip. Using 'Aiki', your aim is to move so your opponent doesn't get a chance to get a good grip on you. This is done by either stepping back and forcing your opponent to reach forward towards you (putting them off balance), or stepping into the attack and striking hard at the same time. Both moves require a finely tuned sense of awareness, and are considered advanced responses. What's more likely to happen is you'll have to defend yourself using 'Ju'. This is more abrupt, and finesse is replaced with brute force. A good Ju Jitsu system will teach you both Aiki and Ju.

>> 1. *Your opponent grabs you with both arms around your arms.*

2. Step back and create a gap. Reach around your opponent's waist with both your arms and interlock hands. If you can't reach your own hands then grab their belt, shirt, or whatever you can.

3. Strike with a short hard knee to the thigh or groin.

4. Step your right leg forward, getting ready to throw.

5. Lift your opponent's right elbow nice and high while maintaining your grip behind their back to unbalance them.

6 and 7. Maintaining your grip, sweep their leg out and throw them to the ground.

Double Lapel Grab

Main Influence: Northstar Ju Jitsu

The ready stance is your connection with stillness. Stillness is ever present, but to feel it you also need to be present. If you are thinking about presence, you are not still. Presence and stillness are not thoughts, and cannot be thought about. The sword cannot cut itself, as the thinker cannot be the observer of the thought.

The best defence against a single or double lapel grab is to move before your opponent gets a firm hold. This series of moves is for when you haven't responded in time, and need to defend yourself with a strong counter using your entire body before a headbutt or other attack follows the grab.

1. From a firm base with your knees slightly bent, bring your arms up and around from your back and over your head in a circular motion. Increase your speed, strength and momentum as you strike down on both forearms to try and break your opponent's grip.

2. Even if you don't break your opponent's grip, you will slightly break their balance and force their arms down.

3. Bring your arms out wide at around hip level.

4. Deliver a hard strike to your opponent's midsection with both fists.

Martial arts and fighting.

I love the combat training in martial arts, not because I like to fight but because it brings out something deep and primal within me. To turn that off, or deny that part of me exists, means I wouldn't be able to express it in a positive and constructive way.

5. Without dropping your arms, follow up along their body (outside their line of vision) and strike the underside of their chin with both fists, forcing their head back.

6. Wrap their right arm tightly in your left arm. Keep their head back with a strike, and push under their chin.

7. Continue with a throw, taking out your opponent's right leg with your right leg and dropping them onto the ground.

Double Neck Grab

Major influence: Northstar Jujitsu, Daito Ryu Aiki Ju Jutsu and Judo

The great black belt will know the right amount of force to use, not too much, and not too little. The only way the black belt will understand this is to be aware of the stillness during combat. They must then train this in every action. You become the martial arts.

The technique starts the moment you enter the dojo and ends when you leave. Everything in the dojo is designed to keep you present. When you are present in the moment, you are living now. This is the essence. This is the truth.

This is a dangerous attack, so the defence needs to be fast and furious.

1. Bring your arms up directly above your head and down onto your opponent's forearms, either breaking or weakening the grip.

2. Bring your arms down and low to give you maximum power.

3. Strike up the middle under the chin, pushing your opponent's head back. At the same time flex your elbows outward to lift your opponent's arms and reduce the strength of their grip.

4. Clasp your hands behind your opponent's head, continuing to lift their arms and opening up their torso.

5. Deliver a short sharp knee to the abdomen.

6. Bring the leg you used to deliver the knee right back and maintain your grip behind their neck.

7. Deliver a front kick to the groin

8. Take your opponent's right hand and clasp it tight, with your left hand clasping the elbow.

9. Take your opponent's arm straight away from your body, controlling it while putting slight pressure on their wrist and elbow to deliver a little pain without forcing it.

10. Continue taking the arm down. It takes skill and control to keep the balance broken.

11. Continue the motion, and draw their arm up so their wrist is above their elbow and your body is 90 degrees or more (but no less) relative to your opponent. Ensure your left arm hugs their right arm like a fire hose, your back is straight, and your legs are apart in a wide stable stance.

12. This is a very strong position of control. If your opponent tries to stand you can simply put all your weight down on their body from your armpit. You can also strike easily from this position while maintaining your grip behind their neck.

Head Lock Basic

Main Influence: Daito Ryu Aiki Ju Jutsu.

Every martial art is MMA. It's nothing new. Modern thinking simply caught up with ancient wisdom.

I've included this as a basic technique. But despite its simplicity it is very much an advanced technique. To make this technique effective you need to be fully aware of the situation you're in and remain emotionally unattached. The difficulty with having these set defences is you can easily be mistaken into thinking they're the end product when in fact they're just a guide. Learn them, train in them, and then forget about them. That way you can be flexible enough in defence to see the attack clearly and then respond, adapt, and deal with the situation using exactly what's needed.

Your opponent swings their right arm around towards you, seemingly to either strike you put you in a headlock.

1. Step slightly away to your left. At the same time, guide their arm. Don't try to block it. By placing the webbing of your left hand at your opponent's right elbow, your aim is to intercept the attack and veer the arm away from you.

2. Duck down without, bending at the waist so you stay upright.

3. As their arm misses you, maintain contact and unbalance your opponent. Watch for their right arm, and counter-attack if necessary by subtly controlling their elbow.

Head Lock

Main Influence: Submission Arts Wrestling (SAW)

You are constantly looking to morph into the space where your opponent is taken completely by surprise.

Before I get into the details of this technique, I just want to touch on my theory of ground defence.

In the beginner phase I don't give students the option of taking the ground. I know many Jiujitsu schools focus their moves in both self-defence and competition on taking the ground as their primary objective. And they're very good at it.

But in my teachings I prefer giving students a thorough education in how to stand and fight before even considering going to ground. Based on my experience, with the correct balance and stable centre of gravity you'll never need to go to ground unless you choose to. As you progress, you're taught how to defend yourself in all ranges of fighting. But you'll always maintain an important and strong base of well-trained striking.

The key to studying all ranges of fighting (including kicking, punching, knees and elbows, standing grappling, throws and takedowns, and ground defence) is to immediately feel your opponent's weakness and exploit it completely. For example, if your opponent is a good boxer you may choose to take out their thighs and groin with low kicks. If you're being overwhelmed standing up you may choose to take the ground. And so on.

Dynamic kicking to where my opponent is the farthest away from me is my first line of defence. To get to my punching, knees and elbows they need to get past my legs. To get to my grappling they need to get past my punching and knees. And to get to my ground defence they need to get past my throwing. Most never get past my legs, and know nothing about my ground skills.

In this case, I choose to go to ground.

1. Your opponent crosses the distance between you and takes you into a headlock. You still have the awareness to be able to respond effectively with Ju Jitsu.

   Stand upright with your feet a little wider than your shoulders and one leg behind your opponent.

2. Take their right hand with your right hand. At the same time, shoot your left arm straight up behind their right shoulder.

3. Crouch down by bending your knees, and put pressure on their right shoulder by bringing it forward.

   Maintain the tight hold of their right hand.

4. Step through with your left leg, continuing to push your opponent down.

5. Take your opponent down completely onto their stomach, pinning them down with a version of kesa gatame (scarf hold). Pin and immobilise their right shoulder.

6. Slip your right arm out, and hold their arm in tight with your left elbow and right hand is if you were holding a fire hose. No submission on their wrist, drill their shoulder into the ground.

Head Lock. Reverse

Main Influence: Submission Arts Wrestling (SAW)

Traditional martial arts are just that, traditional. Most are relics of the past, and only significant from a historical perspective. Traditional martial arts are great for learning the fundamentals. The serious practitioner should then apply that knowledge.

 In this case, I choose to go to ground.

Your opponent has crossed the distance between you and taken you into a headlock. You still have the awareness to be able to respond effectively with Ju Jitsu.

1. Stand upright with both feet a little wider than your shoulders and one leg behind your opponent. Take their right hand with your left and right hand and join your power with theirs.

2. Moving in the same direction of the attack's momentum, slip your head out completely. Hold on to their right arm with your left hand and turn your body slightly towards them. Raise your right arm to shoulder height.

3. Turn and hug their right arm as you would a fire hose (see standard head lock defence), with you right elbow in tight and your left hand holding their right hand.

4. Drop to your right knee, maintaining your grip and control of their arm.

5. Using their right shoulder as a pivot point, slip your right leg down into kesa gatame (scarf hold) with all your weight

6. Once you have control, place their arm down on the ground at least 90 degrees to their body, controlling the wrist and the elbow while sitting back on your knees.

Rear Bear Hug

Main influence: Both Daito Ryu Aiki Ju Jutsu and Tenjin Shinyo Ryu Ju Jutsu.

Watch carefully to see whether the technique is real. Is the attacker being thrown, or are they throwing themselves? Has it become so stylish that it's just another form of dance like the tango?

Because my opponent has such a strong grip, it's too late for me to use Aiki (merging with my opponents power). So I need to use the more abrupt but equally effective Ju Jutsu to break balance.

Break balance. Use the voice. Strike, push and pull. Create pain.

1. You are grabbed from behind around the waist, but your arms are free. Slightly bend your knees, dropping your centre of gravity.

2. Strike with a headbutt using the back of your head. (When training in this technique with a partner, make sure they move their head to the side.)

3. Lift your knee nice and high.

4. Strike down with your heel on to the top of your opponent's foot.

5. Raise your left hand high and away from you.

6. Strike with your knuckles to the back of your opponent's hand. These three strikes may loosen their grip.

7. Take at least two of your opponent's fingers with your thumb and index finger closest to their knuckles. Lift your elbow, taking their arm away from you.

8. Step towards them with your left leg and bring your right hand up to join your left hand, twisting their fingers down and keeping the elbows tight.

9. Keep moving their clasped fingers down so their elbow is on your solar plexus. This will keep the balance broken and your opponent bending backwards.

10, 11 & 12

Bring your left leg forward and sweep your opponent down. Take out their left leg so all their weight is hanging on their bent back fingers.

Rear Collar Grab Outside

Major influence; Daito Ryu Aiki Ju Jutsu.

Most martial arts are just another form of dance. If you think the choreographed routines are the end product of your training, you're hiding behind a curtain of naivety.

How do you know which way to turn? You don't have eyes in the back of your head, and so you won't always know which hand has grabbed your collar. So you need to have defensive moves for both hands and both sides. The basic rule of thumb is to turn and strike, then act. By striking first, it doesn't matter which side has grabbed you.

1. Your opponent grabs your rear collar. Touch and unbalance. You need to act quickly as you can easily be pulled back and down.

2. Slightly turn your head to get a glimpse of your opponent.

   Step forward and across your right foot. Place your right hand on top of your head and your left hand on your solar plexus.

3. Step right around with your left leg and strike your opponent's midsection with the side of your right hand.

4. Bring your left hand down onto their right elbow. This will break their grip on your collar and force them back and down, taking their balance.

5. Keep your left hand on their elbow, and bring your right hand up and strike under their chin.

6. Sweep out their left leg to take them down.

7. As they land heavily at your feet, bend your arm at the elbow and take your fist up and back.

8. Strike down fast and hard, and repeat as many times are necessary.

Front Kick Defence

Main influence: Judo Gene LeBell

There are still ancient Japanese martial arts called kobujutsu that have been passed from master to student for hundreds of years. It's mostly the dedication of non-Asian students that keeps these traditions alive.

1. Your opponent kicks out at you with a strong focused front kick to your midsection. I use a technique the great Judo Gene LeBell taught me: the 'pat and grab'. You don't try to catch the kick. You simply pat the leg, ankle of foot off its intended line.

2. Catch the foot with your right hand. You are out of range of your opponent's counter punches.

3. From a hands up guard, keeping hold of the kicking leg and shoot a straight left punch to your opponent's head.

If you're going to lift one foot off the ground and potentially give up at least 50% of your power, you need to make it count. When you kick someone, it needs to be like walking into a sledgehammer. The kick needs to be direct and to a place that will have maximum effect. It needs to be in and out, with no wasted movement. If you try to kick too hard or too high, you may find yourself on the ground.

The recoil of your kick is just as important as the extension. If the kick lacks focus, it's easy to grab. There are many ways to defend against a kick attack. I've included the kick defence I regularly use.

4. Lifting their leg, grab your opponent's rear collar with your left hand and position your left leg in close against their support leg.

5. Use your left leg and hip to sweep your opponent. At the same time, draw down on their rear collar.

6. Your opponent will drop hard at your feet. Finish off with a punch.

Punch Defence

Main Influence: Northstar Ju Jitsu

I don't follow written doctrine or dogmatic ceremony that replaces the core message. If there isn't a good enough reason to keep it, then just let it go.

1. Your opponent strikes with a straight right punch. Block the punch in close with your left hand. At the same time bring a right punch up under the chin from below the attacking arm.

2. Maintaining control of their right arm, position your open vertical hand on the back of your opponent's neck.

3. Continue to cut down on their neck, forcing your opponent down.

4. Strike with a short sharp right knee.

> Attaining a black belt means you have shown great commitment and dedication to achieving a set goal and an end result.
>
> How you then apply being a blackbelt in everyday life will determine the kind of black belt you become.

5 + 6.
Reach down with your left hand and place your thumb inside the lapel of your opponent's shirt in preparation for applying a choke. Keeping your right hand tight, slide it along the back of their neck and grab your left forearm.

7. Position yourself behind your opponent. While controlling their right arm, apply this very strong choke.

Rear Bear Hug. Pinned

Main Influence: Daito Ryu Aiki Ju Jutsu. Tenjin Shinyo Ryu Ju Jutsu

Ready and still. Everything starts from stillness and finishes with stillness. It is the constant from where everything arises.

"By learning to fight you no longer need to fight". I find this statement difficult. It took me years to get the desire to prove myself out of my system. I prefer to say, "By learning to defend yourself you no longer feel the need to be aggressive".

1. Your opponent tries to grab you from behind. In this attack you can be lifted and thrown onto the ground. So the instant you feel your opponent move your feet so they're shoulder-width apart, slightly bend your knees, relax your shoulders, and breathe. Extend both arms to form a semicircle and test your opponent's grip by slightly raising their arms.

2. While maintaining this stance, rear headbutt your opponent. We are just looking for a distraction that may momentarily cause pain and stun them into releasing the grip.

3. Raise one leg up as high as you can.

4. Stomp down with your heel on to the top of your opponent's foot. Maintain a solid stance, with your arms holding the integrity of the circle.

5. In one swift movement take your opponent's right arm with your left arm, then reach back with your right arm and grab their right shoulder. Place your right leg between their legs, and drop onto your right knee.

6. By dropping down, you effectively take your opponent's balance by creating a hole for them to fall into.

7. Pull your opponent's clasped shoulder and arms to bring them over your shoulder.

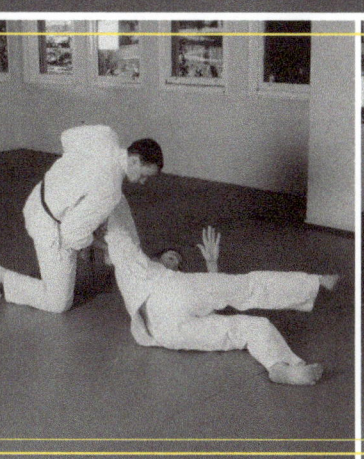

8. ... and onto the ground.

9. With your opponent at your feet, stand up and pull up on their right arm as you raise your own.

10. Deliver a finishing strike.

Neck Grab

Main influence: Taekwondo.

Mindful training. Pay attention to the feel of your feet on the mat, the exact contact area as you hit the pad with your hands or feet, the feel of the uniform on your skin.

1. Your attacker grabs you on the neck. You need to move very quickly, as being grabbed on the neck can be deadly. Step towards the arm grabbing you.

    You need to step in this way, as it will enable you to maximise your defence and attack your opponent's weak spot: their thumb and index finger.

2. At the same time, strike their forearm hard with your right arm to bang it out of the way. Make sure your left fist is on your chin.

3. Turn on the spot and look over your shoulder. Point your hips and get ready.

4. Deliver a rear side kick to a low target. This must be a hard, focused kick. We start off with the low kick to break balance, but you can also kick to the midsection if you have the skills.

Double Shirt Grab. Aiki

Main influence: Daito Ryu Aiki Ju Jutsu

Feel the intention of your opponent. Be still and watch. Intercept their movement and guide it away.

 **Martial arts are a wonderful assortment of moves, strategies and personalities.**

Aikido was developed from Aiki Ju Jutsu and the personality of its founder, Morihei Ueshiba.

Judo was based on Ju Jutsu and the personality of its founder, Jigaro Kano.

Though this defence looks simple, it's quite difficult to get right. Your timing and movement need to be fully switched on.

1. Your opponent steps towards you with their arms stretched out, intent on taking a firm hold of your shirt.

2. Step back so your opponent has to overstretch to get to you. Take your arms in a circle up and over your head, and bring down your arms onto your opponent's forearms or hands.

3. Knock their hands down and continue to do a second circle with your arms. Don't cut this short. The long circular movements are hard for your opponent to see. Bring your hands on top of or just behind their head.

4. Continue to draw your opponent down and strike with a knee.

Double Wrist Grab

Main Influence: Daito Ryu Aiki Ju Jutsu

Too much discipline and you will break. Too little discipline and you become like a winding river, always seeking the easy way out.

The essence of this defence is to move as soon as you feel the touch. Your aim is to defend against the action, not the reaction. So you need to be fully aware and present. This movement will only work if your opponent does not get a firm grip. While their arms are still moving, you intercept their movement so their intent doesn't change. You then join with their momentum and veer the attack into the direction you desire.

1. Move both of your hands out to your side, drawing your opponent forward and exposing their torso.
2. Keeping your arms out wide, deliver a knee strike to their head or midsection.

Single Wrist Grab

Main influence: Tenjin Shin-yo Ryu

Martial arts without etiquette is nothing but a sport.

Martial arts with too much etiquette can be dogmatic.

This series of moves is the next step after you've unsuccessfully tried breaking your opponent's the grip using Aiki.

1. Your opponent grabs your wrist.
2. Leave your hand where it is to maintain your opponent's intent to grab your wrist, and strike their chin with a straight palm strike.
3. This strike should be enough to loosen their grip. Go for the weak point between their thumb and the index finger with your wrist, taking your thumb the full movement up to your opposite ear.

Ground Flow

Main influence: Submission Arts Wrestling. (SAW)

When you feel the need to fight, it is projected from your core, not from your thinking. Your aura is dark, and you will wonder why there is so much aggression around you. Trouble will come to you.

Taking the ground can be a clear advantage. Knowing even a little about how to take control on the ground puts you way ahead of someone who knows nothing on the ground. The following is a ground flow, which demonstrates submission moves. Just keep in mind there may be several people involved. So if you don't want your head used as a soccer ball, take control and then stand as soon as possible.

1. Start by sitting on top of your opponent. Keep your elbows close to your body, and use your opponent's elbow as a pivot point on your solar plexus. Cup their wrist, and draw it up towards their elbow to attempt a wrist lock.

2. Keeping their left arm against your torso, take your left arm with your right hand and push the collar across your opponent's neck in a choke. Come up on your right foot and left knee 90 degrees to your opponent, and push them onto their side with your left knee.

3. In one movement, swing your left leg over your opponent's head. Keep their arm tight between your legs right from the shoulder.

4. Hug their arm with both of your arms, then cross your legs and sit back without raising your legs. This is very important. If you raise your legs, it gives a space for your opponent to escape.

5. Hug their forearm so it's tight against your body. Make it part of your body. Lock their shoulder with your legs without any gaps (you can cross your feet), and slightly raise your hips for the submission.

6. If your opponent manages to clasp his own hands together, sit up while still hugging their arm and keeping your legs in tight,.

7. Keep your left leg across their head to hold them down. Place your right heel into the elbow of their free arm, lean back, and then put pressure on their elbow with your foot to break your opponent's grip.

8 + 9. If their grip is too strong, or they manage to interlock their arms by grabbing their own elbows, lean down towards their legs and take the leg closest to you between their legs behind the knee. (You should still be hugging their arm and have your legs firmly over them,) As long as your grip and position are tight, taking the leg lifts your opponent's head and shoulders off the ground. Keep holding onto their leg, and push down with your own legs until their grip is broken.

Single Shirt Grab

Main Influence: Daito Ryu Aiki Ju Jutsu

Fear will cripple you if you let it grow into a monster. Feel it, acknowledge it, breathe into it. Take a step into the direction you fear.

1. When someone grabs you by the shirt, it's a pretty good indication that things aren't good. The key is to move quickly before they get a firm hold and start hitting you. The passive defence shown in basic grabs is too late.

2. Grab your opponent's hand and hold it in place.

3. Take a step forward with your right leg, keeping your balance even on both legs.

   Regardless of whether or not your opponent pushes you, shift your left leg behind your right leg and bring your right arm up from your hip.

4. Continue to launch your right arm up, striking under the chin of your opponent. They will not see or hear this strike. They will only feel it.

5. Continue through the chin, bringing your arm up high without it going behind your own head.

6. Bring your arm down with a closed fist, and drop your centre of gravity by slightly bending your legs. Strike into the elbow of your opponent. At the same time, start turning their others hand without removing it from your shirt.

7. Bring your right hand up to join your left hand, clasping their hand tightly in your shirt, and continue to turn.

(This motion is called 'kotegaeshi' in Japanese.) Turn their hand and aim to put their little finger on the floor.

8 + 9.

Regardless of whether their hand is still holding you, stand up as straight as you can and strike.

10. Finish off with a knee.

Head Lock to Ground

Main Influence: Submission arts wrestling (SAW)

Why do so many martial artists train for so many years learning to defend themselves? They walk around exuding aggression in their constant state of vigilance. It must be very tiring, but they have nowhere else to go. Learning new skills and perfecting a thousand moves only fills in the empty gaps.

1. You are grabbed in a strong headlock by your opponent.

   Position yourself behind them, and take their rear collar with the closest hand.

2. If they start to strike with their free arm, reach around and grab the upper arm to reduce the impact.

3. Continue with the takedown without delay. Control their rear arm, and step deep behind them.

4. Straighten the leg behind and bend your other leg. Start to pull the back of their collar.

5. Collapse your right leg completely so your entire body weight is on their rear collar, and take them backward onto the ground.

6. Use the momentum from the take down and immediately roll on top to a sitting position on top of your opponent.

7. Take control of a loose arm by taking their left wrist with your left arm, keeping their arm pinned to the ground.

8. Feed your right arm under their left elbow and grab your own left wrist.

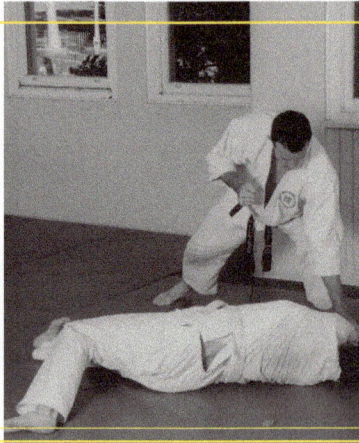

9. Staying in this position, slide their left arm down towards your right knee. At the same time, lift your opponent's left elbow to put a submission on their elbow and possibly their shoulder.

10 + 11.

Push their left arm across their face, keeping the pressure on their left elbow. Stand up and finish off.

Knee Defence

Main Influence: Submission Arts Wrestling (SAW)

The hardest skill to learn in martial arts is killer instinct. This skill needs to be nurtured by the teacher a little at a time. Killer instinct isn't angry or aggressive. It's cold and unemotional. The martial artist who has honed their killer instinct is still and neutral in combat.

1. Become aware of your opponent and your surroundings at the same time. Monitor the space between you. Take a fighting stance, with your weight spread evenly on both legs. Keep your hands down and your shoulders relaxed. Show no emotion, and breathe normally.
2. Your opponent enters your space, clasps both hands behind your neck, and attacks using the knees. In this situation you could easily be pulled down and take a knee to the head.
3. So act fast to avoid being pulled down. Catch their knee with both arms. Stay in front of your opponent, and hug their knee to your body. At this stage you may have been winded, so take a couple of seconds to recover.

4. Maintaining your balance, keep your opponent on one leg. Without changing anything, keep your right arm fixed under their knee and with your left hand strike and push the side of the knee you are holding.

5. As you strike the knee, reposition yourself so you are now side-on to your opponent.

6. Place your left hand into their rear collar.

Zanshin; A constant state of focused awareness. Still and neutral.

Each technique starts and finishes with zanshin. It completes the action. Ju Jitsu without zanshin is not complete. It enables clarity and stillness awareness, so you can be totally present and respond to exactly what's needed.

7. Lift their knee with your right arm, and sweep your opponent with your left leg and hip.

8. Take down to finish off with a strike.

9. Your opponent may hang on, putting you in a head lock. Just go with it and position yourself towards your opponents back

10. Take control by placing both knees on the ground. Prevent your opponent rolling you over by placing both hands down in front of you.

11. Start transitioning from the side of your opponent to the top of them, taking one leg over your opponent.

12. Continue until you are on top and your opponent is flat on their back.

13. Lift your body high enough to slide one of your arms up through the narrow gap between their shoulder and head. Push your arm right through, and then repeat with your other arm.

14. Stretch out both of your arms in front of you with your palms flat to control all movement.

15. Sit up and finish off.

Knee to Throw

Main influence Northstar Ju Jitsu

Hit the pads, the modern day makiwara. Hit the pads in stillness.

Don't have a reason. Don't watch the clock. It's just you and the pads. Give your full attention to the point where the pad meets the fist. This is the working surface. Be one with the pad. This makes your pad workout a spiritual experience, and so much different from a boxing drill.

1. Observe your opponent in their entirety, waiting, still, watching their breath, timing your attack with their in-breath. This is when they are the most vulnerable.

2. When an opening presents itself, move in. Clasp both hands around your opponent's neck and keep your elbows in.

3. Strike with a solid knee to your opponent's mid-section.

4 and 5.

Take your right leg back and, keeping the pressure on the back of their neck, deliver a straight leg front kick between your opponent's legs.

6. If your opponent's balance is broken and they are leaning forward, a throw may be on. Space your legs so they are shoulder-width apart. With your knees bent and your back as straight as it can be, put your right arm around their neck with your fingers pointing towards the ground. With your left arm, firmly hold their right arm in close to your body. Try and get your hips lower than theirs by bending your knees..

At this point, you are facing the same direction as your opponent.

7 and 8.

Straighten your legs and lift your opponent up off the ground onto your lower back. Then cut down with your right arm, throwing your opponent onto the ground.

9. Finish with a solid punch.

10. Step around to the top of their head so you disappear from their view. Keep your hands down as if in ready stance.

11. As they move to stand up, finish with a knee. From zero to 100% and back down to zero in the blink of an eye.

Side Kick Take Down

Main Influence: Submission Arts Wrestling. (SAW)

 My first black belt was in taekwondo. I stayed with my first instructor Tim Hassall after he split from Rhee Taekwondo. My kicking game developed in ways I never could have imagined. But every time you kick, you're giving up at least 50% of your balance. That makes you vulnerable to being taken down.

So as part of the Northstar syllabus, I turned the system on itself and developed ways to counter my kicking with throws. This added an entirely new dimension to the NSJJ system.

1. *Face your opponent in a fighting stance. Adjust the distance between the two of you so they will be tempted to kick.*

2. When they come at you with a rear leg side kick, intercept their kick by tapping and diverting it off its intended line.

3. Catch the kick any where between the knee and the ankle with your other hand.

4. Hold onto your opponent's leg, and shoot a left punch towards their head

5. Take a big handful of their rear collar and step through with your right leg to chamber for a takedown.

6 and 7.

Sweep out your opponent's support leg. Make sure you sweep their leg above the knee.

When a boxer punches, you kick.
When a kicker kicks, you grapple.

The master can recognise the threat and counter into the gaps.

Your opponent will slam face down onto the mat on their stomach. Maintain your hold on their kicking leg.

9. As your opponent hits the ground, step over their leg and place your foot down firmly between their legs.

10. Keeping your leg straight and not bending your knee, use both of your hands (one hand on top of the other) to push their foot from the toes in towards their lower back. Make sure you line up in the same direction as your opponent. and that you are up on your toes on your rear leg.

Kick Defence

Main Influence: Submission Arts Wrestling (SAW)

The turning kick (or the roundhouse kick as it's commonly known) can be devastatingly effective. It can be used against many targets, including low kicks to the thigh, calf, hip, arms, body and head. And unlike its cousin the side kick, it's relatively easy to do. The strike area can be anywhere from the knee to the toes. The shin makes for an awesome weapon when using the turning kick.

1. Your opponent strikes at you using a back leg turning kick.

2. Keep your elbows in close to your body, and take the turning kick on the padding of your upper arm. Lower your centre of gravity by slightly bending your knees. You want your opponent to feel confident and safe that they can kick you without the risk of their leg being grabbed and thrown.

3. Prompt and dare them to throw another kick in the same way. As they do, step out with your right leg and catch their leg with your left arm, securing it. You need to step away from their kick in a circular fashion to take some of the bite out it. Keep your right hand on your chin, locked and loaded.

The ultimate aim of martial artists is to have no aim, no form, no technique, and no "I" that reasons, justifies or judges. All that is left simply "is". Martial arts without form is the same as going to school without textbooks. Lose the form and who will I be? Is training without form the same as not using the form?

4. Strike their head with a right punch.

5. Maintaining control of their right leg, cup your right hand behind your opponent's head. Keep your elbows in tight.

6. Holding their knee up high, step with your right leg in line or just past your opponent's support leg. Make sure you leave a gap between their leg and your own.

7. Come through with your right leg.

8. Sweep their left leg out, drawing down on the back of their collar and lifting their right leg.

9-10. As they drop at your feet, strike hard with a right downward punch.

11. Turn them away from you by discarding the leg you have been holding.

Sparring Drill. Punch to take down

Main Influence: Northstar Ju Jitsu

Surround yourself with the wise. Learn from many sources. Be a person of wisdom. Constantly seek knowledge.

1. Start in a fighting stance with your hands up, your left hand at about shoulder height, your elbows close to the body, and your left hand not too close to your body. The closer your left elbow is to your body, the further your arm has to travel to block and/or intercept a strike.

   Don't stand too square-on to your opponent, as this gives them an easy target. Try and get into the habit of standing more side-on to protect your midsection, with your feet about shoulder-width apart and your right hand on your chin. If you can't feel the hand on your chin, it's too low. Keep your right elbow tight against your body.

2. Initiate movement by edging forward with a left jab to your opponent's head.

3. Lean back and strike with an inside thigh kick with your left leg. This works really well— going from a high punch to a low kick. This kick can also target the groin.

4. Follow with a right cross.

Your right cross is your powerhouse. Learn it well. Make it direct, fast and efficient.

5. Take your opponent's rear collar with your right hand.

6. Slide in behind with a straight right leg. It's very important that you don't bend your right leg at your knee, and that your right leg is down towards their feet.

7. Pulling your opponent's collar downward, bend your left leg and sit down, pulling them down onto the ground. You can now finish this in a number of ways. My preference is to use the momentum of the takedown to roll onto your opponent so you're sitting on top. Then finish.

Single leg take down

Main Influence: Submission Arts Wrestling. (SAW)

Are you a warrior in your dojo but defeated every time you are challenged by life?

The master gets comfortable with hardship and even welcomes it, but does not seek it out.

1. Initiate an attack with a direct palm strike to your opponent's head.

Most of the techniques presented in this book are defensive in nature. Your attacker comes at you, and you then defend yourself with the appropriate moves. Some techniques require you to initiates the attack. This is important to know, as not all Ju Jitsu is defence. Many of the advanced moves will take out your opponent quickly and efficiently. You are striking hard and fast with only the required movement, going from stillness to action and back to stillness, and moving away from any situation with the least amount of fuss.

As your opponent moves their head back

2. ... shoot in under your opponent's arms, placing your left leg deep between their legs. Keep your head on the side of their torso, your back straight as can be, and your left arm around their body. Your right arm should be getting ready to lift your opponent's left leg.

3 and 4.

Continue your forward movement, controlling your opponent. At the same time, step deeper between the legs and lift their left leg as you straighten up.

5 and 6.

Sweep out your opponent's right leg with your left leg, and then lift their left leg.

7. Drop them at your feet. Without bending down too far, strike with a hard punch to the groin.

8. From a semi-horse-riding stance, maintain control of their left leg.

9. In one swift motion, step over your opponent's left leg.

10. Only put their foot down when you've crossed your feet. Try not to make this a two-part step by placing your foot down and then stepping to cross the feet. Place both hands on their ankle, close to the Achilles tendon.

11. Using their leg and their body to cushion your fall, hold onto their leg and sit back, making sure you sit back high on their leg and their leg is straight.

12. Place yourself so their foot is directly in front of your face. Pull their foot towards your face, holding their leg tightly between your legs. You'll know if you're in the correct position as there will be a lot of painful pressure on their knee.

Punch Defence to simple throw

Main influence: Northstar Ju Jitsu

 When you take one leg off the ground you risk losing your balance. This may be okay in sport martial arts such as Judo or BJJ, but for effective self-defence you need to be able to maintain your balance and form when throwing. The simple throw is a distinct Ju Jitsu throw, not a judo throw. The leg leaves the ground to throw and then returns to the ground immediately.

1. Your opponent comes at you with a right punch. Block it with your left arm and catch it under your armpit, controlling the arm by grabbing your own jacket. Strike with a right open hand palm strike.

2. Control your opponent by clasping behind their neck with your right hand, drawing them down and onto your right knee.

It is said that the strong serve the weak.

The master offers service to their students by teaching to the best of their ability, and tempering the speed of education according to the stage of development of the student. Learn to trust the wisdom of the master.

3 and 4.

Maintaining control of their right arm, grab their rear collar with your right hand and thrust forward and down. At the same time, take a big step with your left leg so the heel of your left leg is in line with or past your opponent's right foot.

5. *Without stopping and with one swift movement, lift your right knee up and thrust your right leg deep between your opponent's legs. Strike their thigh with your thigh to take them down*

Punch Defence

Main Influence: Thai Boxing. Submission Arts Wrestling (SAW)

Most martial artists easily give up their advantage and clearly indicate their ability simply by the badge on their uniform. Some wear one badge. Others line their uniforms with several, clearly outlining to their opponent exactly what they've studied and their intention. Your opponent will form an opinion of you in a microsecond based on how you look, talk, walk, and generally hold yourself.

1. Your opponent throws a wild punch. It may be totally unconventional, and nothing like the regular martial arts or boxing punches. But there will likely be a succession of them. Keep your right hand high on your chin, and your left shoulder high to protect the left-hand side of your chin. Thrust your left arm directly towards the shoulder of whatever arm they're punching with, and cup your left hand around the back of your opponent's head.

2. Their punch is likely to glance off your shoulder and make contact with you head. But the intrusion of your left arm will diminish the power of their attack.

3. While your opponent is stretched out their torso is vulnerable to a left knee.

4. Moving in close and keeping your left hand behind their neck, deliver a right elbow.

5. Clasp your hands together around their neck and hold your forearms tight. Pull their head down and strike with a right knee.

6. If balance has been broken and you feel the throw is on, put your right arm around your opponent's neck and clasp their right arm with your left arm in one swift movement. Then slide in so your hips are low (by bending your knees) and your back is straight, and prepare for a throw.

7 and 8.

Lift your opponent onto your lower back and turn your torso by taking your right arm towards the ground.

9 and 10.

With your opponent landing at your feet, finish off with a hard right punch.

Strikes

Strikes are a very important part of any complete Ju Jitsu syllabus. Their importance is often overlooked, with practitioners choosing to focus on throwing and groundwork. Traditionally, strikes were a large part of Tenjin Shin yo Ryu Ju Jutsu. But with the advent of judo, striking became obsolete.

Striking is the quickest and easiest way to break someone's balance. Actually hitting someone is not part of a regular person's daily life. There's always the fringe element who fall outside of this standard deviation—the criminals, thugs and bullies who make violence and suffering part of their daily existence.

As part of a serious study of martial arts, the instructor needs to turn on the average person's instinct to survive. This means cultivating a killer instinct. By doing this, the average person can still be the same, but if necessary will strike out at an aggressor with unemotional ferocity.

What follows are the basic strikes that can be used for breaking your opponent's balance. There are many other strikes that can also be used.

The ready stance

A neutral stance that promotes awareness before combat.

Fighting Stance

Bringing the hands up. Used for offence and defence in combat. I only teach the fighting stance on one side so you get used to blocking and striking while protecting yourself. If you're constantly switching sides it's much easier to be caught out and hit.

Your fighting stance is like your home. It's a safe haven you know you can go to.

Jab

A direct punch in a straight line towards your opponent's centre line. The back hand is tight, protecting your chin. The jab is fast and can stun. I call it a probing technique. It looks for openings so you can gauge how you'll follow up.

Cross

This is your rear hand—the opposite hand to your jab. It's a very powerful technique and can strike hard. Look for the gaps with your jab, then follow up with your cross.

Elbow

A very handy strike in close. Combines well with knees and punching combinations. A favourite of the Thai Boxing fighters.

Palm

The palm heel part of your hand is a very handy weapon. The strike follows the same path as the punches. The only difference is when striking with the palm your hand is open. It makes striking and then grabbing easier to do.

Double Palm

If you're grabbed, strike hard and fast with a double palm strike to loosen any grip. The hands are together, one on top of the other. This is also a very strong move that can be used to push back your opponent's head and chin, and cover their eyes.

Knee

The knee is a very powerful technique. Tremendous power can be generated from up close. It can be hard to see, and even harder to block. If your hands are clasped behind your opponent's neck, you can draw them down directly onto your knee. Knees are especially effective in crowds — short and sharp, with little upper body movement. It all happens below the belt.

Front Kick

When using kicks you need to be cautious and exact. They're very effective for striking outside the punching range, but one mistake and you could end up with a knife between your ribs. The front kick can be used from your fighting stance. Try not to kick too high. Use the heel, toe or ball of your foot depending on whether you're wearing shoes.

Side Kick

The best position to deliver a side kick is with the hips of your kicking leg pointing and taking aim towards your opponent's midsection. Strike with the heel up higher than your toes. Do this and you can be sure you are kicking from your hips/centre and getting the best results. In this photo, my side kick is kicking underneath my opponent's punches.

Groin Kick

The groin kick is a great follow up to the knee strike. It will only work if your opponent's legs are apart. Keep your hands clasping the back of their neck. From the knee, bring the same leg straight up between their legs.

Zanshin

A constant awareness before, during and after any situation you choose. It's especially useful in combat.

Techniques

Ground Control

Your weight is on your opponent's shoulder. Your weight is spread evenly between your legs in a similar way to a kesa-gatame (scarf hold) in judo. Hold their arm straight as if you're holding a fire hose. Drive the arm into their shoulder joint.

Breaking Balance

Putting your opponent in pain will certainly get their attention and break their balance. It's pointless trying to throw someone if their balance hasn't been broken. Without breaking balance it becomes the battle of the strongest, which goes against the principles of Ju Jitsu and Aiki Ju Jutsu.

Throwing

In this photo, an opponent's entire body is being thrown by using their wrist as a pivot point. This throw will only work if you create a hole for them to be thrown into. With their balance broken and their wrist being the pivot point for the throw, your opponent won't be able to defend against a broken wrist unless they go with the direction of the throw, taking the pressure off the wrist by rolling with it.

Stance

Invade your opponent's structure. Stay close, and aim to move into their centre.

Keep your back straight and remain as upright as possible. Don't lean over to compensate. Completely dominate their space. Your opponent will have no choice but to acquiesce.

Pain

In this photo my opponent started from standing. This technique puts tremendous pressure on their wrist. It forces them down and back, like packing them backwards into a box. You need to be careful to not apply too much pressure,

as the pain and damage can be instant. The keys to this technique are to secure your opponent's hand, cut down vertically towards the inside of their bent elbow, and keep the pressure on to take your opponent backwards towards the ground.

Fake throw

When you see someone flying through the air after being thrown, it's easy to think they've thrown themselves and the defence is fake.

Well, it could be.

When someone has been working with one instructor for a while, they may come to understand through repetition how to respond to their instructor's defence. This could mean they throw themselves deliberately to avoid the pain of the defence.

Note: Someone who has no idea what you're doing would just fall to the ground, probably nursing a damaged limb or joint.

Touch and unbalance

Your opponent has grabbed your wrist. With your vice-like grip, the instant you feel them grab you lock their hand onto their wrist to stop them getting away. Use your grip and your forearm to lift them up so your arm is in line with your neck or head. Make their arm straight and horizontal, and apply a painful wrist lock. Maintain the pain and throw.

Maintain good form (part 1)

The end of the technique is important. Make sure your feet are both squarely on the ground., and that your back leg is straight and not bent at the knee. Grip their hand with both of your hands, making sure your grip has no gaps and isn't impinging on their wrist in any way. Moving from your hips, apply pressure down the arm and into the shoulder joint. Don't push so hard that it causes them to bend their elbow, taking the pressure off the shoulder. The translation from Japanese is to use their arm like a spear into their shoulder joint.

Maintain good form (part 2)

Keep your back straight. Don't bend forward. Maintain a deep horse-riding stance, with your weight evenly distributed on both legs. In this photo my right leg is controlling any desire for my opponent to roll away. A deep and secure figure of 4 elbow lock. The pain prevents them from striking me from the ground.

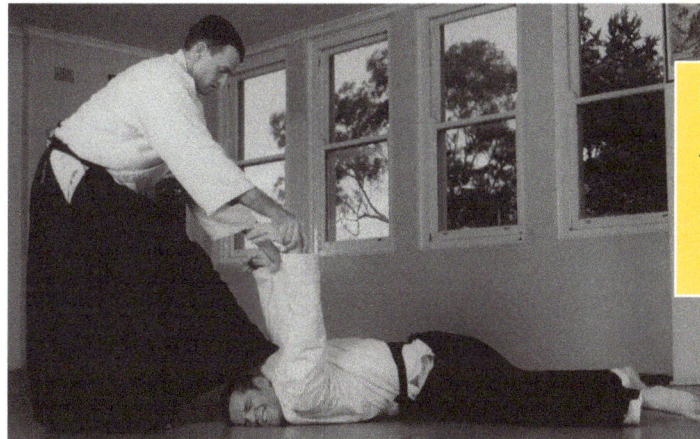

Don't try this at home

A double wrist grab ends with a double shoulder dislocation.

Dangerous technique

Many of the Daito Ryu Aiki Ju Jutsu techniques are dangerous, and unless you know how to fall correctly you can be thrown head first or shoulder first into the ground. It takes exact precision and timing to throw in a way that allows your partner to roll out of the dangerous throw.

Rear Attack

You can learn to become more aware of potential rear attacks. Imagine you're projecting your awareness behind yourself—your energy, your life force. Give it your full attention. Be still and present, and then feel for a signal with your body. Try and move as soon as you feel their presence. It takes practice, but you will be surprised. I get a sensation behind my ear when someone enters my space from the rear.

Chokes

There are many variations of choking techniques in judo and Ju Jitsu. And they're all very dangerous. I rarely teach choking moves because when they're used in self-defence your opponent probably won't know how to submit and can't communicate with you verbally. All you'll feel is the weight of their unconscious body.

Not good.

In this photo I'm using a very powerful rear choke. All of my opponent's weight is backwards, and so they're erffectively hanging themselves.

Complex moves. Keep it simple

This photo was taken towards the end of a defence against a punch.

You're probably wondering how I ended up in this position. It's actually a very nice technique. But who has who?

The longer you stay in the pocket (in range), the more likely your opponent will be able to counter your defence. I may have them in what looks like a superior position, but they also have me as my awareness is held by them.

Blocking a punch

In a perfect world, enter with a block or strike towards your opponent's centre line to counter a straight punch. Then as they vary their punching direction you should vary your defence. Your aim is to block their strike as far away from you as possible. You can then maintain this structure while completing your defence.

In the photo I've blocked a punch well before it has gained any power, strength or momentum.

Appendix 1

Tenjin Shin Yo Ryu Ju Jutsu Shodan (1st Dan) Black Belt Syllabus.

天神眞楊流柔術	TEN SHIN SHIN YO- RYO- JU- JUTSU		
	TE KAZU TO-TARU		124
①	手解	TE HO DO KI	12
②	初段居捕	SHO-DAN I DO RI	10
③	初段立合	SHO-DAN TACHI AI	10
④	中段居捕	CHU-DAN I DO RI	14
⑤	中段立合	CHU-DAN TACHI AI	14
⑥	投捨	NA GE SU TE	20
⑦	試合裏	SHI AI U RA	24
⑧	極意上段立合	GO KUI JO-DAN TACHI AI	10
⑨	極意上段居捕	GO KUI JO-DAN I DO RI	10
⑩	人口呼吸術	JIN KO- KOKYU JUTSU	
⑪	乱捕	RAN DO RI	
⑫	口伝	KU DE N	

① 手解 TE HO DO KI

#			
1	鬼	拳	O NI KO BU SI
2	振	解	HU RI HO DO KI
3	逆	手	GYA KU TE
4	逆	指	GYA KU YU BI
5	片胸	捕	KA TA MU NA DO RI
6	両胸	捕	RYO MU NA DO RI
7	小手	返	KO TE GA E SHI
8	両手	捕	RYŌ TE DO RI
9	気	捕	KI DO RI
10	天	倒	TE N TŌ
11	扱	捕	MO GI TO RI
12	打	手	U CHI DE

② 初段居捕 SHO-DAN I DORI

1	眞之位	SHI N NO KU RA I
2	添捕	SO E DO RI
3	御前捕	GO ZE N DO RI
4	袖車	SO DE GU RU MA
5	飛違	TO BI CHI GA E
6	抜刀目附	NU KI MI ME TSU KE
7	鐺返	KO JI RI GA E SI
8	両手捕	RYŌ TE DO RI
9	壁添	KA BE ZO E
10	後捕	U SHI RO DO RI

③ 初段立合 SHO-DAN TACHIAI

1	行違	YU KI CHI GAI
2	突掛	TU KI KA KE
3	引落	HI KI O TO SHI
4	両胸捕	RYO MU NA DO RI
5	連拍子	TSU RE BYO SHI
6	友車	TO MO GU RU MA
7	衣被	KI NU KA TSU GI
8	襟投	E RI NA GE
9	手髪捕	TA MU SA DO RI
10	後捕	U SHI RO DO RI

Appendix 2

Daito Ryu Aiki Ju Jutsu. White belt to Black belt Japanese Explanations.

Written and formatted by the author. All the intricacies are in these explanations. Sourced from many months of private lessons with Kondo Sensei.

Ippon Dori

Me o Tsuke, Maai o Susumete, Aite no Kokyu o Yonde Imasu.

Aite ga ken de shomen kara Uchi Konde kimasu node

Furi kaburu "In" no toki ni haitte, aite no hiji o tsuki agete,

Seshita shunkan ni Aite o kuzushite, aiki o kakemasu

"Yo" no toki ni akete wa dame desu

Seshita Shunkan ni Aiki o kakeru no wa daiji desu

Chanto aiki o kakeru to, kono jotai desu

Kuzushita mama, aite no hiji no chotto shita no tsubo o osaette

Wakisashi o nuite, yoroi no aite iru tokoro ni nakadaka ippon ken de atemi o iremasu.

Sono toki "to" to iimasu

Migi te wa aite no te kubi o totte

Aite o jibun no tanden no shita ni osaemasu,

Soto miaku o osaete

Sono toki hidari kata wa migi yori sagate imasu

Migi ashi o ugokasanai de, koshi o agezu ni

Aite no wakibara o yari de tsuku yooni shite, kerikomi, koshi o kirimasu

Kimeta mama, atama no ue kara todome no atemi o ire, "Ha to Iimasu"

Aite ga hangeki ga dekinai yoo ni, mada soto miaku o osaete mama

Zanshin o totte, modorimase

Waza wa saisho kara saigo made kikanakereba narimasen, so janai to aite ga itsudemo hangeki dekimasu.

Moo hitotsu daijina koto wa waza o tomenai koto desu

Kuruma Daoshi

Me o tsuke, Maai o sumumete, aite no kokyu o yonde imasu

Aite ga ken o furi kaburu toki wa shomen uchi ka yokomen uchi ka wakarimasen node kanarazu aite no chuushin ni hairimasu

Aite ga henka suru toki ni jibun mo kawarimasu.

Aite ga furi kaburu "in" no toki ni haitte, doji ni nakadaka ippon ken de suigetsu ni atemi o irete

Seshita Shunkan ni aite o kuzushite, aiki o kakemasu.

"Yo no toki ni ukete wa dame desu

Seshita shunkan ni aiki o kakeru wa totemo daiji desu

Chanto aiki o Kakeru to kono jotai desu

Sono toki aite no ryoo ashi no sen no chokaku hookoo ni kuzushite

Aite no kakato no sen yori jibun no kakato o mae ni dashimasu

Sono mama migi te wa aite no kata o totte, hidari te wa aite no tekubi o totte

Koshi o agezu ni jibun no ashi o hikiyose, Aite no kata o oshinagara aite no ashi o harai taoshimasu

Atama no ue kara todome no atemi o ire, "HA" to iimasu

Zanshin o totte, modorimasu

Waza wa saisho kara saigo made kikanakereba narimasen, so janai to aite ga itsudemo hangeki dekimasu.

Moo hitotsu daijina koto wa waza o tomenai koto desu.

Gyaku De Dori

Me o tsuke, Maai o susumete, Aite no kokyu o yonde imasu

Aite ga mune o totte kimasu node

Seshita shunkan ni chuushin o hazushite, aite no shikaku o tsuki

atemi o irete, kuzushite, aiki o kakemasu.

Aite ga mune o tottara, kanarazu tsugi no koogeki ga kimasu node matte wa ikemasen. Seshita shunkan ni atemi o ire aiki o kakemasu.

Shita kara nakadaka ippon ken de migi te wa ago, hidari te wa hiji da Sono toki "To" to iimasu.

Ookiku te o furi agete

Ue kara shita ni migi te wa miken hidari te wa hiji ni uchi otosu

Migi te de, aite no te o tsukande, oya-yubi o koroshite, gyaku ni ko-yubi o kakete, jibun no tanden no shita o osaete,

Sono toki hidari kata wa migi yori sagate imasu

Migi ashi o ugokasanai de, koshi o agezu ni

Aite no wakibara o yari de tsuku yooni shite, kerikomi, koshi o kirimasu.

Migi te wa mada aite no kansetsu o shimete imasu

Kimeta mama atama no ue kara todome no atemi o ire, "HA" to iimasu

Zanshin o totte, modorimasu

Waza wa saisho kara saigo made kikanakereba narimasen, so janai to aite ga itsudemo hangeki dekimasu.

Moo hitotsu daijina koto wa waza o tomenai koto desu.

Koshi Guruma

Me o tsuke, Maai o susumete, Aite no kokyu o yonde imasu.

Aite ga juji o totte kimasu node

Seshita shunkan ni chuushin o hazushite, chidori ashi o funde

Ago o hiki, me o tsukemasu.

Doji ni naka daka ippon ken de suigetsu ni atemi o irete,

Sono toki "to" to iimasu.

Aite o kuzushite Aiki o kakemasu.

Seshita shunkan ni atemi o ire aiki o kakeru no wa totemo daiji desu.

Kanarazu matte wa ikemasen.

Kuzushita mama, migi te wa aite no hiji o shita ni oshi, hidari te wa

aite no hiji o tsuki agete,

Kuzushinagara jibun no koshi o kaiten sasenagara, aite o nagemasu.

Atemi wa atama no ue kara todome no atemi o ire, "HA" to iimasu.

Zanshin o totte, modorimasu

Waza wa saisho kara saigo made kikanakereba narimasen, so janai to aite ga itsudemo hangeki dekimasu.

Moo hitotsu daijina koto wa waza o tomenai koto desu.

Ura Otosu

Me o tsuke, Maai o susumete, Aite no kokyu o yonde imasu.

Aite ga katasode o totte hikimasu node

Seshita shunkan ni sore ni awasete, mae ni denagara, sode o hiki

Doji ni naka daka ippon ken de suigetsu ni atemi o irete,

Sono toki "to" to iimasu.

Kata o irete aite o kuzushite Aiki o kakemasu.

Seshita shunkan ni aiki o kakeru no wa totemo daiji desu.

Kanarazu matte wa ikemasen.

Aite no ryoo ashi no sen no chokaku hookoo ni kuzushite sono toki

aite no ashi no kakato no sen yori jibun no kakato o mae in dashimasu

Kuzushita mama, te o senaka ni mawashite

Kaina o kaeshite, nagemasu.

Atemi wa atama no ue kara todome no atemi o ire, "HA" to iimasu.

Zanshin o totte, modorimasu

Waza wa saisho kara saigo made kikanakereba narimasen, so janai to aite ga itsudemo hangeki dekimasu.

Moo hitotsu daijina koto wa waza o tomenai koto desu.

Karaminage

Me o tsuke, Maai o susumete, Aite no kokyu o yonde imasu.

Aite ga mune o totta toki

Jibun ga Gyaku De Dori ga dekinakatta baai wa aite ga kanarazu tsugi no kogeki o shomen ni utte kimasu.

Karaminage wa saisho no aiki ga maniauwanakatta baai no waza desu.

Ippon dori to onaji yo ni, aite ga furi ageru "in" no toki ni haite, (yo no toki ni ukete wa dame desu)

Seshita shunkan ni aite o kuzushite aiki o kakemasu.

Seshita shunkan ni aiki o kakeru no wa totemo daiji desu.

Chanto aiki o kakeru to, kono jotai desu ne.

Kuzushita mama empi ga hairenai yo ni hiji no shita no tsubo o osaete

Soto miaku o osaemasu.

Shita kara nakadaka ippon ken de atemi o irete, sono toki "to" to iu.

Te o totte juji ni karamete nagimasu.

Nagete kimeta mama hiji no shita no tsubo ni kakete

Atemi wa atama no ue kara todome no atemi o ire, "HA" to iimasu.

Atama no ho ni itte

Zanshin o totte, modorimasu

Waza wa saisho kara saigo made kikanakereba narimasen, so janai to aite ga itsudemo hangeki dekimasu.

Moo hitotsu daijina koto wa waza o tomenai koto desu.

Obi Otosu

Me o tsuke, Maai o susumete, Aite no kokyu o yonde imasu.

Aite ga juji o totte kimasu node

Seshita shunkan ni chushin o hazushite chidori ashi o funde

Ago o hiki, me o tsukemasu.

Doji ni naka daka ippon ken de suigetsu ni atemi o irete,

Sono toki "to" to iimasu.

Aite o kuzushite Aiki o kakemasu.

Seshita shunkan ni atemi o ire aiki o kakeru no wa totemo daiji desu.

Kanarazu matte wa ikemasen.

Kuzushita mama, migi te wa obi o totte,

Hidari te wa aite no migi ude o mochiage kuzushite

Ago o tsuki agemasu

Ookiku ippo dete, otoshite,

Atemi wa atama no ue kara todome no atemi o ire, "HA" to iimasu.

Zanshin o totte, modorimasu

Waza wa saisho kara saigo made kikanakereba narimasen, so janai to aite ga itsudemo hangeki dekimasu.

Moo hitotsu daijina koto wa waza o tomenai koto desu.

Kiri kaeshi

Me o tsuke, Maai o susumete, Aite no kokyu o yonde imasu.

Aite ga Ryoo sode o totte kimasu node

Seshita shunkan ni chidori ashi o funde, chuushin o hazushite

Aite o kuzushite, Aiki o kakemasu.

Seshita shunkan ni aiki o kakeru no wa totemo daiji desu.

Chanto aiki o kakeru to, kono jotai desu ne.

Aite ga modoroo to suru tokoro o riyoo shite hairimasu.

Kuzushita mama, migi te wa atama no ue de,

Hidari te wa aite ni miichaku shite, kaina o kaeshite

Ushiro ni nagemasu.

Atemi wa atama no ue kara todome no atemi o ire, "HA" to iimasu.

Zanshin o totte, modorimasu

Waza wa saisho kara saigo made kikanakereba narimasen, so janai to aite ga itsudemo hangeki dekimasu.

Moo hitotsu daijina koto wa waza o tomenai koto desu.

Kotegaeshi

Me o tsuke, Maai o susumete, Aite no kokyu o yonde imasu.

Aite ga ryoo te kubi o totte kimasu node

Seshita shunkan ni te o hiraite

kashi wa de o utte

Te kagami o tsukutte aite no hiji o nobashite

Aite o kuzushite, aiki o kakemasu

Chanto aiki o kakeru to aite wa kakato o ue ni agemasu

Kuzushita mama

Te o shita kara koyubi no tsukene o osaete, gyaku ni oyayubi o totte

Jibun no koyubi o kiriyorosu yooni shite

Sono toki jibun o ude o nobashite aite no hiji o ku no ji ni shimasu

Sono mama mata ue kara kiritoashimasu

Aite no ude o aite no atama ni michaku sase

Hiji o oshi, sono kekka, aite wa koshi o agemasu

Koshi o ageta jotai de

Atemi wa atama no ue kara todome no atemi o ire, "HA" to iimasu.

Zanshin o totte, modorimasu

Waza wa saisho kara saigo made kikanakereba narimasen, so janai to aite ga itsudemo hangeki dekimasu.

Moo hitotsu daijina koto wa waza o tomenai koto desu.

Shihonage

Me o tsuke, Maai o susumete, Aite no kokyu o yonde imasu.

Aite ga ryoo te kubi o totte kimasu node

Seshita shunkan ni aite o kuzushite aiki o kakemasu

Seshita shunkan ni aiki o kakeru koto wa totemo daiji desu

Chanto aiki o kakeru to aite wa kakato o ue in agemasu

Sono mama ude o nobashite, nuki do ni haite,

Ookiku kuzushimasu.

Kuzushinagara jibun no chuushin ni torinagara,

Tai o kaette, te kubi, hiji, kata no sanka sho o kimemasu.

Sono mama nagetara aite no ude ga oreru node

Te no uchi o yurumemasu

Yurumeta jotai de kesagiri ni nagemasu.

Atama no ue kara todome no atemi o ire, "HA" to iimasu

Zanshin o totte, modorimasu.

Aite ga ryoo te-kubi o totta toki, te o mae ni dashimasen.

Jibun no te wa kanarazu jibun no karada ni tsukete okimasu.

Waza wa saisho kara saigo made kikanakereba narimasen, so janai to aite ga itsudemo hangeki dekimasu.

Moo hitotsu daijina koto wa waza o tomenai koto desu.

Appendix 3

Andy Dickinson
Northstar Founder

1979	Commenced Training Taekwondo (Rhee)
1984	Achieved Black Belt East Coast Taekwondo
1984	Commenced teaching Taekwondo. Hiscoes Gym
1986	Commenced Training Tenjin Shin Yo Ryu Ju Jutsu
1988	First Non Japanese student to be accepted into Daito Ryu Jutsu
1989	Achieved Black Belt in Tenjin Shin Yo Ryu Ju Jutsu in Japan
1989	Commenced Judo at Sydney University Dojo
1989	Graded to 2nd Dan Black Belt Taekwondo WTF Reg # 5037921
1990	Accepted into Australian Society of Ju Jitsuans (government recognized body for Ju Jutsu)
1990	1st Place Australian Ju Jutsu Championships
1990	Competed in World Ju Jutsu Championships USA
1991	Lived in Japan for 12 months intensive training in Daito Ryu Ju Jutsu and Submission Arts Wrestling. (SAW)
1992	February - Completed Level 1 Coaching Accreditation in Ju Jutsu (General principles, generic coaching. Sports specific for Ju Jutsu)
1993	Graded to 3rd Dan Black Belt Taekwondo WTF
1994	Achieved 3rd Kyu in Judo

1994	Accepted into Australian Taekwondo Union
1994	Accepted into Guild of Australian Black Belts
1996	1st Australian to be graded to Black Belt Daito Ryu Aiki Ju Jutsu in Japan
1996	Elected Vice Chairman of World International Sports Ju Jutsu Assoc. (ISJA)
1996	Accepted as the head in Australia for the International Sports Ju Jutsu Assoc.
1996	Captain and Coach of Australian Sport Ju Jutsu Team. (ISJA)
1996	Competed in World Sports Ju Jutsu Championships USA. (ISJA)
1996	Received award from International Sports Ju Jutsu Assoc. for Recognition or Outstanding Service to Ju Jutsu
1997	Graded to 4th Dan Black Belt Taekwondo
1998	1st Place at British Grand Prix Champion of Champion Tournament
1998	Captain and Coach Australian Sports Ju Jutsu Team competed World Championships Canada
1998	Ranked no. 5 World in Sports Ju Jutsu. (ISJA)
1998	1st Place All Japan Ju Jutsu Championships
2000	Captain and Coach Australian Sports Ju Jutsu Team competed World Championships, England.
2002	Accepted into Taekwondo Australia as a full voting member (Government body for Taekwondo in Aust.)
2002	Completed Level 1 CHISM Certification Program Children's Hospital Institute of Sports Medicine
2005	Founded Northstar Martial Arts, Sydney.

2008	Graded to 2nd Dan Daito Ryu Aiki Ju Jutsu in Japan. Kondo Sensei.
2008	NCAS Level 1. TKD Australia
2009	Graded to 2nd Dan Submission Arts Wrestling in Japan. Aso Sensei
2009	Promoted to President (9th Dan) of the International Budo Ju Jutsu Federation Japan. Under IBJF Chairman Aso Sensei (10th Dan)
2011	Developed and implemented the CRM system Business of Motion, a complete prospect, membership and payment hub for small business
2013	Current active member count - over 1000. Current trainer count - 36
2013	Head Coach for Australian Team competing in World Championships Poland Nov 2013 International Sports Ju Jutsu Association. 4th Place Teams.
2013	Founded Northstar Ju Jitsu.
2014	Awarded Certificate 4 in Martial Arts
2015	Graded to 5th Dan Taekwondo WTF Kukkiwon
2016	Graded over 140 Black Belts in Northstar Ju Jutsu
2019	Awarded 8th Dan in Sports Ju Jitsu by the World Sports Ju Jitsu Organisation. Poland.
2019	Authored Book "Stand Tall" and author of 9 ebooks.
2020	Launched 2 online subscriptions: jujitsuanytime.com and the Mastery Academy.

Acknowledgements

A huge thank you to the heavyweight champions that gave me such raving testimonials, Patrick McCarthy Hanshi, Sensei Philip Hinshelwood, Tom Cronin, David Nowland.

To all my teachers who walked beside me, lighting my path with their wonderful knowledge and guidance.

To my brothers - John, who shared many parts of this great journey with me, and Rob, for helping me believe I can do anything I set my mind to.

To all the trainers and students at Northstar Ju Jitsu for trusting me to light their path on the incredible journey we walk together.

And especially to Liz, my rock, and Tom, my oak.

About the Author

Andy is the founder and head of Northstar Ju Jitsu. He has spent over 40 years training, competing and researching all aspects of martial arts and personal wellbeing worldwide. He is passionate about teaching martial arts as a legitimate path to understanding oneself and helping his students to see the link between training in the dojo and living a courageous life.

He has written and recorded a thorough online academy that adds a new dimension to the quality of how martial arts is taught and allows Northstar Ju Jitsu to be studied anywhere in the world.

The author of *Stand Tall* and several eBooks, and a prolific blog writer, Andy presents and educates on a multitude of topics related to martial arts and life. Above all else, Andy finds his greatest inspiration teaching all levels of students and nationalities on his online academy.

https://www.facebook.com/Andrewgeorgedickinson

Instagram/andydickinson

www.andydickinson.com.au

www.northstarmartialarts.com.au

www.ingramcontent.com/pod-product-compliance
Ingram Content Group UK Ltd.
Pitfield, Milton Keynes, MK11 3LW, UK
UKHW061203180426
11947UKWH00031B/2067